Bristol Radical Pa

Tremors of Discontent

My Life in Print 1970-1988

Mike Richardson

ISBN 978-1-911522-59-1

Bristol Radical History Group. 2021.
www.brh.org.uk
brh@brh.org.uk

In memory of

Christine Richardson (née Maull)

1948–2015

Contents

***Bristol Evening Post*, 20 February 1986**

Swap row union boss is fired

By Norman Crossland

A UNION officer at DRG Flexible Packaging, of Fishponds, Bristol, where 95 people have been made redundant has been sacked.

Mr Mike Richardson, the father (chairman [sic]) of the SOGAT 82 clerical chapel (office branch) had refused to leave the job he had held for 14 years and to take the place vacated by a redundant employee.

He will take his case to an Industrial Tribunal.[1]

Introduction

In May 1986, the chair of my Industrial Tribunal hearing put the question: "Why on earth should a 39-year-old man with a wife and two children, employed at the company [DRG Flexible Packaging] for fourteen years, take such an action without good reason?"

He was right; my family would suffer economically, and it had been difficult for me to explain and justify my act of refusal to them. But I was clear in my own mind—how could I agree to take the job of one of my members, who the company had declared redundant, and who I had been elected to defend? Compliance with the company's directive would have destroyed my personal integrity, honour and conscience, at home, the workplace and in the wider trade union movement.

I had not automatically come to hold such strong principles. Like many others in my generation, I had moved from a vague sense of rebellion as a teenager in the 1960s to a wider awareness of class inequality in capitalist society and had slowly become a socialist. The immediate consequence of my actions was to be a period of unemployment followed by a series of low paid casual jobs with poor working conditions. Far worse though was the feeling of mental isolation which accompanied losing my job and contact with the people I represented in the Society of Graphical and Allied Trades (SOGAT).

For many years I have felt the need to record and reflect on how it was that I became a union activist in the printing and packaging industry and what formed the anti-capitalist outlook I still retain. While there are many academic studies of workers' resistance and consciousness during the 1970s and 1980s, few accounts relate the personal-political experiences of activists like me. Concentrating on the significance of lived experience humanises the narrative.[2] Moreover, the day-to-day work of lay union representatives over an extended period of time is rarely the subject of examination. *Tremors of Discontent* explores how my own individual consciousness came to change. It shows how gradually my participation in the union and left politics broke through my boyhood reserve, detachment and low self-esteem. External political, economic and social circumstances in the 1970s and 80s intensified this process.

I have checked my memories with written evidence and drawn on several oral interviews with the people who I had worked with to fill in any gaps that I could only partially recall. I present them chronologically, in a narrative documenting my early life, my experiences as a trade union representative in the 1970s and 80s, my association with revolutionary politics and the events that shaped my thoughts and actions. In this way the reader can follow the growth and development of my convictions and beliefs and of the responses of the people with whom I interacted closely.

My personal story was far from unique. I hope my particular account can contribute to a greater understanding of how militant social and political views came to be held by thousands of other rank-and-file trades unionists in the 1970s and 80s. And I hope it will encourage others to share their memories more widely.

Chapter 1

My Early Years

I was born in Bristol during the big freeze of March 1947 to working-class parents, James and Doreen, who, along with many others, were struggling to support their family at a time of rising prices and the lack of affordable housing. Rationing had been introduced in 1940, after the German invasion of France and the Low Countries had signalled the end of the 'phoney war'. Initially it covered food products, fuel, coal, clothes and soap; in the post-war period it had been extended to include bread for the first time. In the harsh winter of 1946-1947, there was an acute shortage of domestic coal upon which most homes depended for both heating and cooking.

To add to my parents' anxieties, my father, like millions of demobbed men, found it difficult to secure steady employment at a wage sufficient to keep the family. As for my mother, coping with looking after my four-year-old brother, David (Dave), and me, fell on her shoulders, for in my family the centrality of the male breadwinner was not questioned. My parents both accepted customary assumptions about the personal roles of men and women.

Nevertheless, they were affected by the social changes introduced by the post-war Labour government. After I was born, my parents were given notice to vacate the flat they rented, so their housing needs were reassessed by the Bristol Corporation. With two children, and under notice to quit their privately rented property, they moved quickly up the public housing waiting list. Not long afterwards they were given the keys of a council house, one of the hundreds built after the war on the new Lockleaze estate in the northern suburbs of Bristol.

The design and layout of Lockleaze owed much to one of the pioneers of town planning, Raymond Unwin, who in turn was influenced by William Morris, the artist and poet, and Ebenezer Howard, a proponent of garden cities. Such links had become remote. Unaware of how our house had come about, we children quickly adapted to the new sense of spaciousness. Made of thick concrete walls, our semi-detached three-bedroom house, with a bathroom and separate toilet, was a great place for my older brother Dave and I to play hide-and-seek, with its built-in cupboards and wardrobes. By climbing over a fence at the bottom of our large back garden, we had access to a large field, flanked by some mature trees, which led down to the main Bristol to Gloucester railway line. Finding ourselves able to run free, and along with our friends, we took full advantage of it. Also, being near the railway line, we could collect train numbers, a popular hobby in the 1950s.

We loved to explore and would sporadically venture out beyond our estate. In seeking adventure, one of our favourite haunts was Snuff Mills on the banks of the river Frome in Stapleton, north Bristol, around two miles or so from our home. On one occasion, along with several children aged between eight to fourteen, and led by my elder brother, we set out on an expedition to the Mill, exploring the woodland on either side of the river. We tied ourselves together with a long rope in order to keep together and not lose any of the younger ones. On reaching the woods, however, we had to abandon this plan as it proved impossible to manoeuvre through the trees.

During this escapade we encountered a strange man around 40 years old dressed in a smart blue suit. As I recall he said he was Canadian. He spoke to us about a collection of stuffed animals that he had, such as owls and other birds of prey, and promised to send us some if we would leave our names and addresses. A girl who lived just round the corner from us, in Landseer Avenue, did provide him with her details, but I don't think any of the rest of us did. Frighteningly, a few weeks later two children, June and Royston Sheasby, aged seven and five, were found in a shallow grave in the undergrowth of the wooded embankment of the River Frome near Snuff Mills. They had been brutally murdered.

A week or so later police detectives conducted house to house enquiries in the surrounding areas, gathering any information that might provide a clue. My mother answered the door, and Dave and I were stood behind her. She said she could not help them and as the detectives turned away, we reminded her that we, along with other children, had recently been in those woods on our expedition. She ushered us in telling us to be quiet. She never explained why she was so reticent to share this information with the police. Nor do I know whether other parents in the street, when questioned, also remained silent on the matter. I can only wonder if it was a mix of fear and shame, both of which haunted my mother all her life. This incident has stuck stubbornly in my memory. The murderer was never found.

Ironically the real danger arose for my brother and me, not from venturing into the countryside, but from within our own home. Soon after taking possession of their new council house, to make ends meet my parents took in a lodger, a middle-class army friend of my father, who was to remain for several years. Council tenants were meant to get permission from the local authority to take in lodgers, but many did not, including my parents. He helped my father landscape the garden by erecting a trellis, making a fishpond, and laying lawns separated by a concrete path and crazy paving border. While he seemed helpful and friendly, behind this façade lurked a malevolent man who, throughout my childhood, took every opportunity he could to sexually abuse me. Confused shame kept me silent, damaging my self-esteem. I was subsequently to learn that he had similarly molested my older brother, who eventually confronted my parents on the matter. He then disappeared from our lives entirely, though the memories of this evil man continued to plague us.

I received my early education at Filton Avenue infant and primary schools. Though not in Lockleaze both were within walking distance from my home, across the other side of the railway line. Despite being in the top class at junior school I struggled to keep up with my peers. I was anxious and each day I used to count my worries—something that has stayed with me. Nevertheless, in 1958, I passed my eleven-plus, as my brother, Dave, nearly four years my senior, had done before me. I was one of those borderline children who had to attend a viva, which consisted of two assessors, a man and a woman. I cannot recall their questions, but I do remember telling them a story which my aunt had told me, about how terrified she had been when a hurricane struck while she was living on an army base with her GI husband in Florida.

I do not know what criteria they judged me on, but I ended up being placed at my local secondary modern school. Situated on the edge of the estate, Lockleaze School was designed and built to provide education for a growing new community. Initially, 11- to 16-year-old children were given places at the school; this was to be extended a few years later to include 16- to 18-year olds by the creation of a sixth form.[3]

Aged eleven, I was put into one of the two grammar streams but, unlike my elder brother, who would go on to study at Queen Mary University in London, over the next five years I found it difficult to keep up and maintain the standard of work expected of a 'selected' pupil. I never seemed to have enough time, or the desire, to do my homework. I failed to make the grade. In my school reports during the early 1960s, my mathematics tutor described me as "lazy"; my English teacher said, "I worked quietly, but with no great enthusiasm"; and my history master

Michael (Mike) Richardson 1963.

stated that "I was out of my depth and thoroughly idle".[4] I was shy and introverted, and drifted aimlessly through school. It was as if school somehow passed me by. I went in regularly but was never quite 'there'. It was not true however that I was idle. I just didn't get it.

My world outside school was, in contrast, all too real. From the age of fourteen I had an evening paper round, a stint of around one and a half hours, and, from the age of fifteen, a Saturday morning butcher's round, a physically taxing job on a clapped-out old bike with a front carrier, dodgy brakes and no gears. I still remember my dread of getting out of bed in the early morning, though I never missed a Saturday during the winter of 1962-63, one of the coldest on record. Many of the side roads and pavements were covered with deep-lying snow from January to March.

Customers paid for the meat on delivery, and thus I was responsible for collecting the money. During this cold spell my hands were often freezing, making it difficult to handle cash. Sometimes, I had to ask customers to do it for me. I really appreciated the kindly ones who invited me in for a cup of tea, but in truth I just wanted to get on and finish my round. I felt driven as if I was in combat with time. I remember bitterly resenting the butcher creating new tasks, such as getting change from the bank, on the occasions when I managed to get through my round early. I also had my first brush with the law. One Saturday morning I was stopped by a policeman for riding my butcher's bike on the pavement outside the shop in Gloucester Road. He took my name and address and, a few days later, he came to see me at home to interview me about my 'misdemeanour'. My guilt was established, and I received an official written cautionary warning from the court.

In the school holidays I would also occasionally help my father on his round as a driver salesman for the Birmingham brewery company, Davenports. He used to deliver beer to people's homes, operating out of a depot in Stokes Croft, Bristol. This experience brought me to parts of the city where I would not normally have gone. As late as 1960, bomb sites still existed in central districts such as Broadmead, Old Market, St Philips, St. Pauls and Easton, while the effects of partial demolition of rows of boarded-up disused houses, during slum clearance programmes, were plain to see. In assisting my father, I came across homes under multi-occupation by West Indian immigrants in search of a better life, who later became referred to as the 'Windrush generation'. I remember their rooms being sparsely furnished and in a state of disrepair. The areas were run-down and many of the dwellings were unfit to live in. Despite the lack of facilities on our council house estate, their harsh living conditions and poverty seemed remote from what my family and I enjoyed.

This 'other world' in the central districts of Bristol rarely attracted attention in the local newspapers. Nor did I ever hear, either at school or at the church, which my parents compelled Dave and me to attend, of the injustice meted out to British citizens from the West Indies who had exercised their right to enter, settle, and work in Bristol and elsewhere in Britain. At the time I did not observe any irony in Lockleaze School virtuously campaigning and collecting funds for the world-wide Save the Children Fund. But I do remember the publicity in 1963 surrounding the campaign against Bristol Omnibus Company's policy over its refusal to hire Black or Asian bus crews.[5]

On Sundays, though our parents were not practising Christians, Dave and I were sent off to St Mary with St Francis, the High Anglican Church in Lockleaze. For me the positive feature of going to church was that it allowed me entry to its youth club. This is where I mixed with my peers, girls and boys, mostly white. We had fun, playing records, dancing, and generally socialising. At the end of the evening, some of us would break into couples, which often led to a boy 'walking' a girl home. I was fifteen when I began to take a special interest in a girl at the club with thick lovely dark hair and beautiful brown eyes. I had seen her in school before, and though I had never spoken to her I felt drawn towards her. Her name, I learned, was Christine Maull and she was fourteen.

One evening at the club, while we stood around the record player listening to music, she slid her hand across the table gently touching the tips of my fingers, sending a warm sensation through the whole of my being. I was surprised and yet somehow filled with certainty; I walked her home that night! From then on, we became a couple. Perhaps a little concerned about close associations forming between adolescent boys and girls, the Church brought in a Christian woman who lectured us, not on the practicalities of sex, but on the difference between love and infatuation. I was fascinated. I remember spending some time writing a résumé of what she said, adding some notes of my own. The intensity of my response did not connect with any interest in religious faith, but simply came from a desire to understand.

Although several of us in the youth club went to confirmation classes, we never really took them seriously. Annoyingly, these classes often clashed with inter-school chess matches. I had learned how to play the game through my father and older brother. It had become a source of fascination and I began to show some ability. Unfortunately, to get to these chess matches on time I had to leave my confirmation classes early. The remote and censorious vicar, Reverend Leslie Jones, would scowl at me, showing his displeasure on my premature departure. At the confirmation rehearsal ceremony, we giggled and laughed throughout because it felt so strange and unreal, though on the actual day we put on a stellar performance.

More memorably for me, during this period, the church youth club hall was chosen as one of the locations for filming the movie, *Some People* (1962). Supported by the Duke of Edinburgh youth award scheme this film, written by John Eldridge and directed by Clive Donner, sought to counter images of delinquent British working-class teenage culture in the early 1960s. It starred Kenneth More, Ray Brooks, Anneke Wills, David Hemmings and Harry H. Corbett. I became one of the many extras used in the shooting of one of the scenes, which took place in the youth club hall.

One particular sequence, performed in St Mary with St Francis' Church, turned out to be an event uncannily similar to one I had actually taken part in with several school friends, some of whom were choirboys. In the film, Ray Brooks climbs the narrow spiral staircase leading to the church organ high up in a chamber. He enters and starts to play rock and roll music while his mates below, one clothed in a white cotton choirboy's surplice, jive to the sound, only to be interrupted and admonished by the vicar. A few months before this film was shot, my schoolboy friends and I had similarly ascended the same stairs, and after reaching the chamber we too had attempted to play some recognisable music, but with little success. We removed some of the smaller organ pipes and placed the tips into our mouths and blew as hard as we could, as though we were playing tin whistles, creating ear-shattering shrill tones before we carefully returned them to their appropriate slots. Despite the din we did not get caught! To this day I have no idea if we were heard or whether the scene was just a coincidence.

I left school in the summer of 1963 with one 'O' level in Greek Civilisation! I was one of the few that passed. It had been one subject that had engaged my curiosity, partly because of the teacher's enthusiasm. After taking my exams, although I was given some formal guidance on exploring career options and opportunities, I had no idea actually how to go about finding a job. I wandered around aimlessly looking for work in the hope that something would turn up. After a couple of weeks, I happened to walk into Jones' Department Store (now Debenhams), in Bristol, to see if they had any vacancies for shop assistants. After completing an application form, I submitted it with my school testimonial, which somewhat surprisingly, painted me in a fairly good light:

> [Richardson] has shown particular ability to work quickly and his progress and industry have been quite satisfactory...
>
> Richardson will prove to be a reliable young person to employ, capable of showing a notable degree of conscientiousness and initiative in his duties.

On the strength of this, I was called upon to attend an interview with Ms Clutterbuck, the personnel manager. She offered me employment as a trainee sales assistant, which included one day's release each week to study stage one of the National Retail and Distribution Certificate (NRDC), a qualification introduced in 1951.

Dressed in a new brown checked suit with a single-breasted jacket and yellow striped lining, for my first day at the store, I clocked in to register my time and attendance record and, with several other recruits, enrolled on and began a week long induction programme. We were taught customer service skills and learned about security matters, handling money, issuing refunds and operating the tills. While we received information on the work, the organisation and the management structure, the possibility of access to union or non-union employee representation was not covered. I knew little about trade unions.

The week after induction I was taken to the second of three floors to meet the head of the wallpaper and paint department, where my first experience of a full-time permanent job began. I still have a vivid memory of the section head, Ivor Bodey, frequently arriving for work breathless from the effort of his journey, because he had previously been a builder and had to retire on ill-health grounds. He introduced me to the other unit members. Among them was Ron Young, a former painter and decorator, and Margaret Cox, an in-store representative for the old Bristol paint and varnish manufacturing company, Colthurst and Harding. Later Margaret, who was around the same age as my mother, kindly organised a private tour of their factory for me, which was on the Bath Road in Bristol.

The staff on the adjoining do-it-yourself section included a few other boys a year or two older than me. In this group was Andy Pickford who I would come across again in the early 1980s during the struggle against the attack on trade unionism by Margaret Thatcher's Conservative government. By then Andy had become a shop steward representing members of a trade union in the printing and paper industry, at the DRG carton factory in Fishponds, Bristol. This was a subsidiary of the Dickinson-Robinson Group (DRG) that was just across the road from where I was to work.

At first, I settled in well at the department store, making new friends and getting involved with the social scene organised by one of the personnel staff. I was chosen for the athletics team to compete against our sister store, Bonmarché in Gloucester. I came second in a 100 yards race and won a Ronson cigarette lighter for my efforts, which says much about the times! On another occasion I tried my hand, with others, at brass rubbing at a church in east Bristol.

I enjoyed working in the store and became increasingly interested in painting and decorating, and the skills and tools associated with it. I loved listening to the stories told by Ivor and Ron of their life experiences in the trade. However, I was unenthusiastic about the NRDC course, which focused on making a career in retail; after grudgingly completing stage one I decided not to move on to stage two. Around this time, the store's management started to put pressure on me to cut my 'Beatle-style' hair to what they termed as a 'respectful' length. Regardless of my earlier lack of confidence, I was a young 1960s worker and did not accept that they had the right to dictate the length of my 'precious' dark brown locks.

I assumed I could find other employment, and indeed, soon after I handed in my notice in January 1965, I was in a job at the paint, wallpaper and tools counter at Thomas Cox and Sons, a builders' merchants at Whiteladies Gate in Clifton, a real contrast to the department store. Double glass panelled doors provided the main access to the shop and we faced customers entering from behind a glass counter on which stood a hand operated till. Behind us were shelves stacked with paints of various colours and sizes ranging from half-pint tins to gallon cans. A selection of tools was displayed in the two large plate glass windows. Wallpaper pattern books were available on request. A yard at the rear, with access to lorries and cars, contained building materials. One of the first skills I learned was how to trim the protective edges of wallpaper reels on a hand-operated machine.

Though the shop served both trade clients and the general public, our core customers were jobbing builders, many working on the maintenance of Clifton houses and flats for letting. I was impressed by the skills of the builders, carpenters and decorators I came across during that time, and watching and listening to them concluded that I would have done better to learn a trade through an apprenticeship scheme, directly after I had left school.

In marked contrast to the large department store, there were only two of us in the shop, the decorating supplies manager, 56-year-old Jack (John) Burris, and me. Jack had previously run his own retail paint and wallpaper business in Gloucester Road, Horfield, near to the butchers where I had worked. He was a heavy smoker and every few days he would send me to the local newsagents to buy his cigarettes, 40 *Woodbines* and ten *Capstan Full Strength*. The picture I still have of Jack in my mind is of him with a cigarette dangling from his lips and brushing off ash from his clothes. He came to act like a father figure towards me. He used to trust me with the shop's keys so that I could open up in the mornings and take the cash float from its hiding place from behind some tins of paint and empty it in the till. This enabled him to attend to his wife, who had cancer, without being under pressure to get to work on time.

On the whole I enjoyed the job and stayed there for nearly three years. Nevertheless, at quiet times it could sometimes feel quite oppressive working with just one other person, but when there was a constant flow of people in and out, conversing, seeking advice, making purchases and occasionally logging complaints, it created a lively environment because Jack continued to behave as if he was running his own business.

I watched one dramatic incident with Reverend Vyvyan-Jones, who at the time was the Labour Lord Mayor of Bristol. He had come in and bought a consignment of paint for a church project, which he placed in the back of his van. On driving away from the shop, he had to brake suddenly. Tins of paint were thrown across the floor of the vehicle, the lids popped off and the contents spilt out. He returned to the shop in a rage claiming that the damaging spillage had resulted from the loose-fitting paint lids. But Burris remained unabashed. He gave the Reverend Lord Mayor short shift, angrily dismissing his accusations by asserting that the 'accident' had happened off the premises.

Though I was picking up knowledge from my jobs, I had as yet no experience of a collective workplace or political resistance, there was nonetheless a more personal rebel mood among some of the friends I had grown up with. Outside of work, in 1966, I teamed up with an old school mate, Mike Dauncey who, with some of his pals, came up with the idea that we should buy an old jalopy good enough to get us to Catalonia and back—a round trip of over 2,000 miles. For the purpose, we bought a second hand faded blue Bedford van with sliding doors for £60. It had no side windows, no rear seats, a dicey engine and no spare tyre. We put an old double mattress in the back for comfort, drove down to Portsmouth, and caught a ferry to Le Havre.

On our way down through France to Catalonia, we frequently had to stop to top up with oil, as well as petrol, because the engine kept overheating. It did not really occur to us that it was in danger of seizing up completely. Apart from a puncture, however, we had no other major delays, and arrived safely at our chosen destination, Lloret de Mar, where we stayed for a week or so and then moved on to a campsite close to Barcelona. Mike was the creative force behind this 'adventure'. Best described as an anarchistic individualist, he was a likeable, pleasure seeking rebel who did not readily submit to authority.

Although I was nineteen years old at the time of this trip, I had little knowledge of social and political matters, either nationally or internationally. Unlike some of my contemporaries, I had failed to register what the Vietnam War was all about, and I knew nothing of Spain's civil war or Franco's authoritarian regime that was still in power during the 1960s. While in Barcelona we met and socialised with a couple of young American sailors returning from US operations in Vietnam; and I remember that we bellowed "Franco is a bastard" in a deserted part of the city in the middle of the night. Yet I remained indifferent to the implications of this brush with wider political polarities between fascism and the left.

* * *

In March 1967, just before my twentieth birthday, I married Christine Maull. Chris was my first love, and we were both utterly committed to one another. There was a certain defiance in our courtship and marriage. My parents and Christine's father told us we were too young; the disagreeable vicar of our church, Reverend Leslie Jones, did everything he could to stop our relationship. Hence, we were left with no option but to marry in a church from a different parish and paid for our wedding without financial help from our parents. Marriage to us represented freedom to live as we wished.

Of course, things were not easy. We did not find a place to live until two weeks before the wedding when we moved into a rather dilapidated, unfurnished, lower ground floor flat in Coronation Road, Bedminster, at a rent (including rates) of £3 10s a week, around a quarter of my income. With the help of my father, we repaired, cleaned and decorated it. We bought some new furniture with money we had saved and a generous £50 gift from my parents. My kindly boss, Jack Burris, gave us an antique television set and a pair of large butter knives with ivory handles, which have lasted much longer than the TV.

We wanted to save a deposit for a house. But foolishly, I left the builders' merchants without securing other work. My plan had been to search for a job with higher pay. Again, I thought that this would be relatively easy. I was wrong. This became evident when I guilelessly attended an interview for a machine assistant at an engineering shop, wearing a black suit, a white shirt and a tie. As I walked through the open yard approaching the factory, young women and girls in a separate workshop whooped mockingly as I passed by, giving them some light relief from their everyday routine. I did not get the job. I found myself situated awkwardly between the demarcations of manual and white-collar work, and thus belonging in neither.

As a consequence of not filling any social category I ended up being worse off by having to take work at the Bristol Co-operative Retail Society (CRS) distribution warehouse on slightly less money than I had earned at the shop. Any hope of getting a mortgage on our joint wages was remote, for at best in the 1960s mortgage companies would only take a portion of a married women's wage into consideration when applying for a loan. My only option was to borrow twice the amount of my salary and some of Christine's income. Even this only allowed us to borrow up to a maximum of £2,000. Realising this was not enough in June 1968 we gave up and spent some of our savings on a package holiday in Greece.

I still had little understanding of international affairs and was largely unaware of the seriousness of the 1967 non-constitutional coup d'état in Greece. The British government's decision in 1968 to enter into diplomatic relations with the Colonels' new regime had meant that their seizure of power was being condoned in Britain as legitimate. No

Mike & Christine (Chris) Richardson 1969.

mention of it was made on the tour, though I was to learn that many Greeks still held bitter memories of the Nazi occupation in World War Two. On our two day coach journey from Milan down through what was then Yugoslavia and onto our final destination, Athens, the Greek woman who was our tour guide referred with considerable emotion to the wartime suffering in which Greeks had died, not simply from combat but through mass starvation. This made Heinz, a sandy-haired young German, born after the war, anxious, and several of us sought to ease his feelings of guilt and discomfort.

A couple of months after our return from holiday, Chris fell pregnant. And in April 1969, much to our delight, she gave birth to our first child, Amanda Jane, in Walker Dunbar hospital, Clifton. The hospital was named after Eliza Walker Dunbar one of the first women in Europe to qualify as a medical doctor. By coincidence it also happened to be a stone's throw from where I was born, in Mortimer House.

In 1969, men were not usually allowed to be present at the birth, though I could and did attend some antenatal classes. Chris chose not to breastfeed, which enabled me to participate more closely in the care of Amanda. We prepared formula milk for her 24 hours in advance. I used to do the night and early morning feeds, and nappy changes, and Chris did the rest.

We applied to the local authority for a council flat and were placed on the waiting list. Several months later, we were fortunate in obtaining one in Dancey Mead, Highridge, south Bristol, about four miles from the city centre, a side of the city with which I was then unfamiliar. At the time I was employed as a clerk at the National Dock Labour Board (NDLB) in Hotwell Road, and rather than having a short walk to work I now had to rely on public transport or a lift from a colleague.

In this period, I registered for a correspondence course to study Maths, English Literature and English GCE 'O' level; I scraped a pass in the former two but failed the latter (twice). I moved swiftly from job to job. Prior to working for the NDLB, I had been an order picker in the CRS distribution warehouse, serving its food sales outlets. I left the NDLB after six months to work at the Royal Mail sorting and delivering letters. After a three-month stint on night and early morning shifts, I walked out to take up a job as a clerk at the wine merchants of Dudley Smith in Queen Square.

Though I did come across unions in some of these workplaces, they remained remote to me. The CRS, for instance, had a pre-entry closed shop agreement with the Transport & General Workers Union (TGWU), thus as a condition of my employment I had to join. Problematically, the union was completely inactive at the warehouse where I was employed. We had no representative, and no union official visited the site in the year that I was there. Health and safety concerns would frequently arise without being adequately dealt with.

On one occasion, in frustration, a work colleague and I feigned an accident in an attempt to draw attention to the dangers we often faced. We pulled over a pallet loaded with boxes of canned beans that were balanced precariously on the edge of a high rack. Quickly my friend covered me with some of the boxes that had come crashing down and shouted for help. When the supervisor arrived on the scene his first concern was to see what damage had been done, not to me, but to the goods, remarking; "it's a good job these weren't glass." I dusted myself off and said I was unhurt but complained about the peril of having to climb stacks in order to get at some produce because there were not enough forklifts and trained operatives to go round. Nothing was done.

Aged 23, poorly qualified and my confidence low, any hope of obtaining higher paid employment, without having to work excessive hours was very unlikely. Only my Royal Mail job had paid anything like a reasonable wage, though I had to work seventeen consecutive twelve hour nights over the 1969/70 Christmas period. This was followed by weeks of long working days since I was doing up to four hours compulsory overtime ('docket' as it was called by postal staff) per shift, to cover a shortage of staff due to a flu epidemic. As a result, I had little time with Chris and Amanda; I knew I could not keep on like this.

My mind was racing one cold snowy winter's morning in January 1970, while on my post round in Stockwood, on the outskirts of Bristol. As I passed a pillar box, I stopped, turned round and then, impulsively, deposited the remaining letters I had to deliver in it. I then marched to the nearest post office and handed over the outstanding parcels. I cycled home, changed my clothes, took my postal uniform and postbag to the main sorting office, and handed in my resignation with immediate effect.

Within a few days I got the office job at a wine merchants in Queen Square, but on lower wages. Chris managed to obtain part-time, weekend casual work, as a cleaner at motorway service stations and caravan parks. But as a couple with a young baby, we were finding it hard to survive. We were just scraping by and I worried about what to do. Whereupon Mike, my old rebel school friend, told me I should apply for a position, at his place of work, in the production control office of the flexible packaging arm of the Robinson Waxed Paper Company (RWP) in Fishponds, Bristol. RWP was a subsidiary of DRG.

Following two interviews, one with the personnel manager, Jeremy Procter, and one with the production control manager, Ken Shipton, I was employed in the sample order office. This was the division within production control that scheduled the manufacture of modified and new flexible products for the company to test and for customers to trial. Under close supervision I was taken on to progress chase sample orders through their varying production processes, which included physically transferring sample reels from one production process to another until completion. This entry into regular employment with a large firm introduced me to a complex workplace and contact with a wide range of people. It acted as the catalyst, which was eventually to draw me into trade unionism.

Chapter 2

In the Deep End (1970–1972)

1970

When I arrived at the Robinson Wax Paper Company, in the spring of 1970, it employed around 1800 people. The firm converted raw materials into various forms of flexible packaging. It produced a wide range of printed and plain flexible packaging products, mainly in reel format but also pouches and sheets supplying both food and non-food market sectors. Its customers included large companies such as Cadbury Fry's, Kraft Foods, Kodak, Lever Brothers, London Rubber, Nabisco, Polaroid, Procter and Gamble, Rowntree and dozens more.

It had built its business in the inter-war years on producing plain and printed waxed paper, suitable for machine wrapping sliced bread. This was still the case when I joined the company; printed on an ancient flexographic press and then processed on a 1930s rudimentary industrial dip-waxing machine. For a brief period in the early 1970s, when this press was short of work, it printed disposal paper knickers that were popular for a short time! A far cry from printing bread wrappers specially designed to celebrate the coronation of Queen Elizabeth II in 1953.

The company ran a two-week induction programme for all new employees, office and factory, every few months. I was put on the programme soon after I was taken on. It began with a brief overview of the company's history. Then we had a guided tour of the factory and were addressed by a supervisor and manager (or deputy) from every production department and given a health and safety briefing. This provided us with a grounding of what each department did. The induction also included a brief account of the role of trade unions given by one of the shop stewards. By the end of the programme, we had collected plenty of handouts, which I put in a file to consult over the months ahead. I found most of the sessions useful. They were well designed and engaging.

I had never worked in a factory environment before. Navigating my way around was like moving through a maze, and I soon realised that familiarising myself with the technicalities, routines and flows of work in the production process would take some time to master. It did, however, present a challenge because grasping its structure as a dynamic entity enabled you to see how each activity interconnected with others. Gradually I was able to map it.

The factory was divided in two with a private road, within the boundaries of the company premises, passing through the middle. On one side was a three-storey building (No. 2 factory); on the ground floor were flexographic and gravure printing presses, lacquer and glue laminating machines. Housed on the second floor was the finishing department, containing several slitting and rewinding machines, with varying specifications. These cut large reels of printed (and plain) paper, film and film/foil down to a number of smaller coils ready for packing and despatch. The supervisors' office was in the centre, raised a few feet off the floor, panopticon style, which gave them all round vision to monitor the workforce. On the top floor were pouch and bag making machinery, roll-fed sheeting machines for cutting printed paper and the sorting and packing department which, in contrast to all the other departments, was largely staffed by women. Also, on the second floor in this building were offices, a plant room (containing pipework and mechanical and electrical equipment), a Dixon pilot coating machine for running trials and an artist design studio. On the third floor there were more offices and a research laboratory. At the far end, and on the same side as the three-storey factory complex, was the ink and lacquer store, the work-in-progress repository and the boiler house and chimney.

Across the other side of the dividing road at the front, facing out onto the main thoroughfare, was a three-tier glass-fronted office block that was set back from the main road behind a grass verge and a hedgerow. On the ground floor was a reception area and offices for middle management, their secretaries and meeting rooms. The production control, buying and sales staff, along with typists, secretaries and post room personnel, populated the middle floor. A hubbub of human activity in these departments reverberated with the noise of people progress-chasing their orders. In contrast, the wages and accounts departments, which occupied most of the third floor, were relatively quiet. Also, on this level, at the far end, the directors had their own waitress/waiter service dining room, the cost of which, including food, was borne by the company.

Behind the offices was a single-floor workshop divided into three main sections (No. 1 factory). The first section had a glass roof encrusted with algae and bird droppings. It housed wax coaters and laminators, emulsion coaters, slitting machines, one flexographic press, and a packing and storage area. Situated in the middle section was the paper,

SPOOL

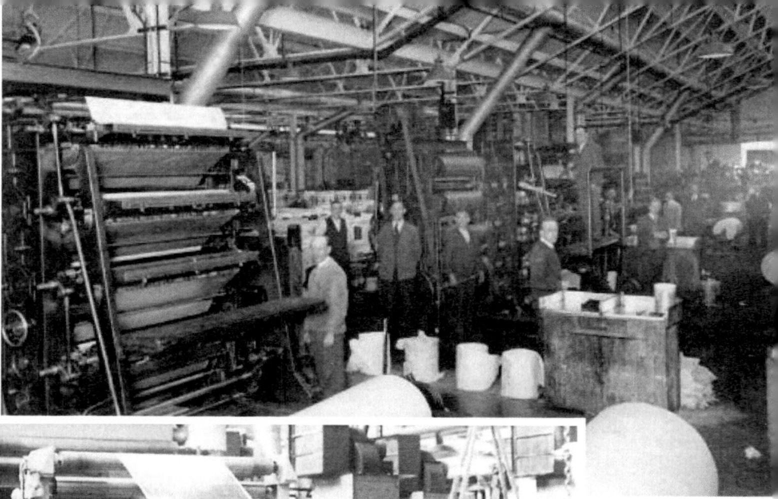

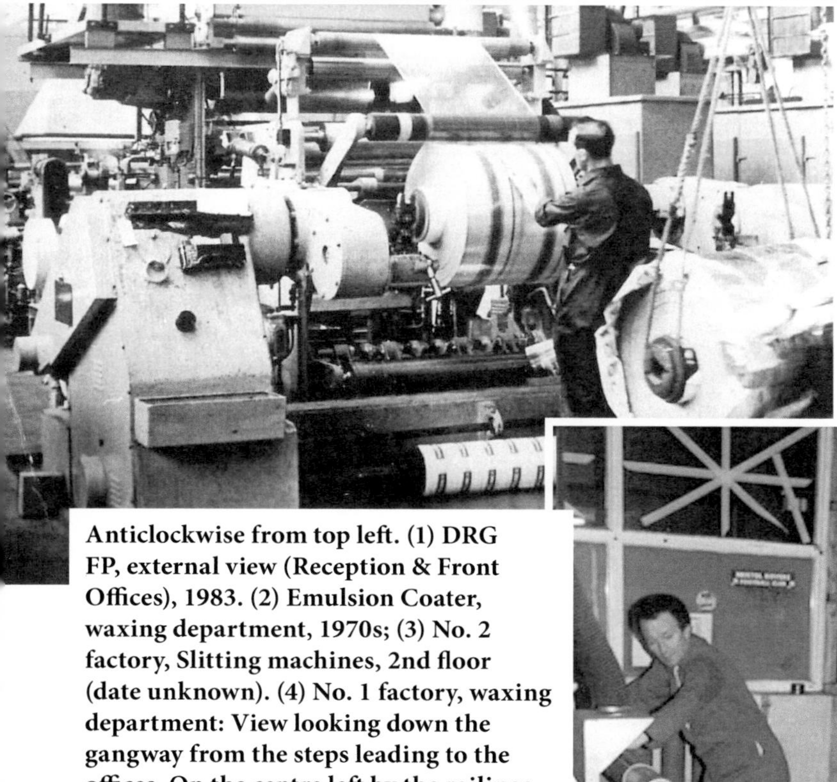

Anticlockwise from top left. (1) DRG FP, external view (Reception & Front Offices), 1983. (2) Emulsion Coater, waxing department, 1970s; (3) No. 2 factory, Slitting machines, 2nd floor (date unknown). (4) No. 1 factory, waxing department: View looking down the gangway from the steps leading to the offices. On the centre left by the railings is a dip-waxing machine (W.3). On the far right at the back is a flexographic printer (F.1), 1970s. (5) Waxed Paper-Making Machinery at Robinson Waxed Paper (RWP) Company, 1930. (6) RWP/DRG FP Polythene Extruder (PE2) 1970s. (7) RWP Foundry stereo relief rubber printing plates mounted on rollers, 1970s.

film and foil store, the general store, the waste corner, the cutting room where spools were pared to size for receiving the slit reels, the quality control product testing laboratory and the foundry; here the stereo relief printing plates, cast from rubber, were attached with double-sided adhesive tape to rollers which would eventually be used on the rotary flexographic presses. The third section, the polythene department, contained three large polythene-extrusion machines, a few slitters, a supervisors' room on a side wall along with a few administration offices. Beyond this was the engineering workshop. Up a flight of stairs to a second floor were the works canteen and the staff restaurants.

The meals were free for senior staff in their restaurant. Office and shop floor employees had to pay for their food. Moreover, although their self-service canteen was on the same floor as the senior staff restaurant, a partition wall divided them.

In the 1970s, class boundaries, while beginning to blur in society, were still culturally overt in the company. Various forms of distinguishing workers in differing positions persisted. Most shop floor employees, including quality control, were engaged continuously on double or treble shifts. The office staff worked days from 8.30am to 5pm, covering multiple functions in production control, estimates, sales, marketing, buying, wages and accounts. The same schedule applied to the typing pool, secretarial undertakings, post room, reception, despatch, and the switchboard.

Despite the differentiations, our interconnections were apparent. For instance, when I started in production control (before it was moved to the front offices on the second floor, a year or so later) it was situated on the second level, above the lacquer and glue laminating machines. The heat, the low frequency noise and vibrations, coming from the machines operating below, penetrated the room and sometimes, caused excessive sweating of one's feet. There was also a constant low-pitched humming noise coming from the nearby plant room.

I was assigned to the sample order office that was on the same level but across the way, on the opposite side of a dividing staircase. Ron Perry, a former supervisor in the factory, with over 40 years' service, was my section head. Ron had been transferred to the office, sometime before I started, as a result of allegations against him of bullying and intimidation brought by some machine operatives in his department. I soon became aware that the factory floor unions had some clout and would not be pushed around. But my own impression of him was of bluster and blather, rather than of bullying. I remember my friend Mike Dauncey playfully wrestling with him in the office, which ended up with both of them rolling on the floor laughing.

Three others worked in our office, two men and a woman. One of them, Ivor Bush, was a founder member of the National Society of Operative Printers and Assistants (NATSOPA)[6] clerical chapel (union workplace branch) at RWP. Ivor spanned the two worlds of manual and white-collar employment. Some years before he had been employed on the shop floor, but after an accident in which he lost part of a finger, the company relocated him to the office.

Established in 1965, the clerical chapel had been formed largely as a response to the decline in the traditional advantages, in terms of pay and status, previously enjoyed by RWP's white-collar staff over their blue-collar colleagues who had been unionised since the factory opened in 1928. Progress was slow as its membership was never sufficiently numerous to have an effective voice. The ambiguous class position of clerical and administrative staff had inhibited the growth of the clerical chapel throughout the 60s and would continue to act as a constraint in the 70s and 80s.

Not long after I started with the company the chapel began a recruitment drive with the goal of reaching a high enough percentage of office workers to bolster its claim for a closed shop agreement. Mike Dauncey, who had introduced me to the firm, would not sign up, probably because his rebel personality inclined him to disregard most rules and any form of authority. When the clerical chapel secretary, Derek Williams, asked me to join, I declined. I do not exactly know why. It was not for any ideological reasons. I was just not accustomed to working in an active trade union environment. In my previous jobs there had either been no union presence, or the union representation had been removed and bureaucratic.

I liked Derek, a quiet, unassuming but principled young man. He was a keen footballer and played in one of the RWP teams. In 2009, I interviewed him to find out how he became active on the clerical chapel committee. By this time Derek had studied at night school, gone to university and had become a lecturer at Southampton Solent University. He told me that he had started with the company in 1968, a couple of years after leaving Withywood School in south Bristol. A crucial difference between us was that, unlike me, he had come from a union family. Derek's father had been an Amalgamated Engineering Union

(AEU) shop steward at an engineering factory in the 1940s and 50s. So, he had grown up with an understanding of unionisation.

When I entered the company in 1970, Derek was employed in the order office, where the atmosphere was easy-going and fun. Even when he made errors, such as putting the wrong colour ink on an order, which cost the company thousands of pounds, he only received an unofficial warning. Subsequently though, he was to be transferred to the stock records section where, in stark contrast to the freedom he had enjoyed in the order office, he came under the watchful eye of a fastidious anti-union section head. He still carried on with his trade union responsibilities, despite receiving flak, even from some union colleagues, for having time off to attend meetings with management.

He described how he, and other chapel committee members, had faced the problem of organising a cluster of heterogeneous clerical workers with a range of differing attitudes towards the role of trade unions. On one occasion, in the early 1970s, when Derek asked my office colleague, Ivor Bush, who had been with the company since he was a boy, whether he would come out on strike over a pay claim. He replied, "I am a union man but I'm an RWP man too."[7] This kind of dual loyalty was common among those members of staff, mainly male, with long service records. But the younger men tended to be more restless. Mike Dauncey was soon to leave while Derek would depart in late 1973.

I happened to arrive at RWP when unionised staff had, for some time, been unhappy because the company had not taken their petitions seriously. Several unions, with diverse traditions depending on whether they represented craft or non-craft workers such as clerical staff, were active in the company. The key players were the craft union, the National Graphical Association (NGA), and the non-craft unions, NATSOPA and SOGAT. Since the 1920s, all three unions had had a closed shop agreement with the company (meaning that all employees had to belong to an approved trade union). This covered the factory floor workers, and this was where the union's strength at RWP had been established. They were well organised and had effective lay representatives in all departments and on all shifts. The Society of Lithographic Artists, Engravers and Process Workers (SLADE), representing the artists and designers, also had a closed shop. However, this agreement did not extend to clerical staff, some of whom had voluntarily joined NATSOPA to reduce their individual bargaining weakness in petitioning company management for better pay and conditions.

Instead of real collective force, there was a marked lack of deference among some of the younger staff like Mike Dauncey. On one occasion, after we had listened to a state of the business talk by our office manager, Ken Shipton, Mike made his protest. Because of the falling level in the company's profits, we were informed that staff had to cut down on the unnecessary use of stationery such as pens, pencils and paper clips. Mike returned to his desk and, in a mocking gesture, tossed handfuls of paper clips around the office. To the relief of some of the older staff, who found him too high-spirited, loud-mouthed and discourteous, Mike left the company several months later. We remained in touch for a few years and I went to see a few of the pioneering liquid psychedelic light shows that he put on at the Old Granary Club in the centre of Bristol and elsewhere. Then after training, he went on to become a highly regarded television lighting camera operator, working on documentaries such as Arena ('Tales of Rock 'n' Roll: Walk On the Wild Side', 1993).

Mike was not alone in finding humorous send-ups more appealing than unions. From the early 1960s, the company had recruited up to 30 school leavers every September, a good proportion of whom were assigned to administrative work such as accounts, wages, sales, and planning. They livened up office culture, particularly in the production order office, and were not intimidated by hierarchy. One trick the order office supervisor fell for on several occasions was the swapping of the internal and external receiver and transmitter handsets so that he would pick up the wrong phone to answer. Another was fastening the switches on the base unit, where the handset rested with adhesive tape, so the phone would continue to ring whenever the receiver was picked up. These generated hoots of laughter.

By the early 1970s, office attire as well as attitudes to authority was changing at RWP. The baby boomer generation being more confident than their predecessors expressed themselves at work through their clothes. Some men in their early twenties challenged the unwritten rule of wearing suits and some went tie-less. Some of the younger women wore short skirts and, one or two, hotpants. Even the men wore more fashionable and colourful clothes. I recall being ribbed by shop floor workers for wearing an open-necked, lime green translucent shirt.

Despite continuing gender inequality, shifts were occurring. In June 1967, two years after its formation, the clerical chapel elected two women representatives, one from the accounts office and the other from production control, onto the chapel committee. By the time of the passing of the Equal Pay Act in 1970, supposedly prohibiting unequal pay and working conditions between men and women, the clerical chapel had around 20 female members.

Employers insisted that they needed time to adjust. Thus the 1970 Act did not come into force until 1975 and, as elsewhere, women employed at RWP continued to suffer from pay discrimination. Their average pay at this juncture ranged between 72 and 80 per cent of that of their male counterparts on work of equal value. Nevertheless, despite facing some managers who were openly hostile to reform, by 1970 the clerical union, in its short life, had secured some minor victories such as sick pay, a women's rest room and the abolition of having to clock in and out of work.[8]

When I first arrived, I was unaware of the struggles RWP clerical workers had had in gaining union recognition and extracting from the company small improvements in working conditions. My ignorance of the rumbling discontent of lower paid staff and the clerical chapel's struggle to better their working lives contributed to my lack of interest in the union. So did my own situation. My earnings were notably higher than in the previous jobs I had held, and I had chances of promotion to higher graded work.

An opportunity for advancement came quicker than expected. When, a few months after the Conservatives' general election victory in June 1970, a vacancy opened up for a production scheduler. Ken Shipton ignored the convention of advertising the post. He called me into his office and told me that after two weeks training, I would be taking over the production planning of orders to be carried out on a range of flexographic printers, waxing coating and wax laminating machines.

This was a short period in which to digest the requisite technical knowledge. I had to understand the printing and waxing processes so that orders were produced on time, on suitable machines and to the required standard, in ways that met the practical and economic requirements of production. This brought me in contact with a range of staff from senior managers to account executives. Similarly, I was working in close cooperation with the shop floor, managers, supervisors, machine operators and assistants, as well as workers in the ink, wax, paper, film and foil stores, in order to discuss and, where possible, resolve any problems that may have arisen. This involved assessing their likely impact on the production plan. By chance I had landed in an intermediary position, moving between the different workforces. This was to be extremely educative. It sometimes meant that I was faced with several conflicting predicaments and perspectives.

In a more removed sense, I was also exposed to the processes of inter connection which made production possible. I had never before experienced this kind of complex, large scale 'cooperation' at work. Planning production made me aware of the inner workings of the firm and to see that the way 'cooperation' was set up was tilted markedly towards the benefit of the employers. So, it was then not just the large scale of my workplace, but also the specific character of the job I did, which led me to question this disparity.

1971

Dramatic events in society at large also impinged on me, as they did many others. In January 1971, not long after I had settled into my new position, the printing unions instructed their members to support a one-day strike against the Conservative government's Industrial Relations Bill. This Bill was designed to handicap the unions from taking industrial action by increasing the role of the law in regulating industrial relations. Paradoxically, the government's action brought politics into the workplace.

Tensions ran high. The number of industrial stoppages in Britain had reached a record level by the end of 1970. Though the clerical chapel was divided, the majority supported the strike call and on 12th January walked off the job to attend a half-day protest gathering in central Bristol. But some members stayed at work objecting to what amounted to a political strike. Ken Shipton summoned non-union people like me into his office to inform us of the event, implying that it was of little of consequence. I remember a feeling of embarrassment as the strikers donned their coats and left the building. This discomfort remained and, combined with my exposure to the social relations of production on the shop floor, it was to erode my indifference to unions. I felt impelled to put vacillation aside and join the clerical chapel.

However, another three months passed before I was enrolled with the union.[9] My delay in signing was due to a mini crisis in the clerical chapel triggered by the half-day stoppage. Dave Sturges, who worked in the wages office, and was then the elected senior union representative, known as the Father of the Chapel (FoC), resigned in protest over the union's directive to strike against the Industrial Relations Bill. Those members who had refused to walk out on the day of action supported him. This disagreement turned into considerable animosity, with the result that Dave Sturges eventually left the chapel. Later, the company appointed him as a section leader in the accounts office.

The conflict over the January strike was to have long-term repercussions. Some chapel members had become disillusioned as a result of Sturges' resignation, and for a while the functioning of the chapel was disrupted by the crisis, weakening its position vis-à-vis management. However, peace was eventually restored after a young man from the accounts office, Malcolm Howard, stepped forward to take over as FoC. A Buddy Holly look-alike, down to his thick rimmed glasses, Malcolm played the guitar in a local pop group. He was a quiet person, who got on well with everyone he came in contact with. He was diplomatic and self-confident, though members outside of the accounts office rarely saw him.[10] In contrast to production control staff, his job largely confined him to his desk.

After the election of Malcolm, aside from work related matters, day-to-day talk in the staff areas returned to normality. In production control, the usual topics of conversation were office politics and leisure interests, such as travel, gardening and, for men, sport dominated. The factory, including the staff and middle management, ran inter-departmental skittle, football, and cricket teams, all of which were very popular among men, and were the subject of endless banter and analysis when time and opportunity permitted. The women did establish a netball team and I remember playing against them in a seven man squad one summer's evening in the early 1970s. None of these sporting pursuits attracted me that much, and anyway living on the other side of the city made it difficult for me to participate. So, I remained somewhat outside the informal social networks. However, I did once run the line as an assistant referee in an inter-office staff men's football match.

RWP seemed to favour familial recruitment, which commonly served to strengthen these networks. It was not unusual to find that staff members, both in the offices and the factory, were related. In our offices for instance there were a father and a son, a mother and daughter, four sets of brothers, one pair of sisters, and a young woman and a man whose fathers worked on the shop floor. Some romantic relationships among the staff blossomed into marriage too.

In theory these close connections might seem to contribute to cohesion, but this was not necessarily the case because disagreements between family members could become more personal and intense. For example, union membership was a contentious matter between one pair of brothers, Mike and Des Mulligan. Des was anti-union and Mike was a loyal union member, and they both worked in the same office! There were all kinds of mysteries. Des, who had been demoted from management, had a mysterious knack of always seeming busy, though what he actually did was never clear. I used to observe other senior staff practising this devious skill without ever comprehending quite how they actually contrived the illusion of diligence.

Not only was I not particularly interested in participating in RWP's sporting activities but also I did not live locally, or have any family members at the company. My feeling of being an interloper was accentuated because my particular pleasure came from playing chess. Nobody I met at RWP shared my interest; indeed, they found it rather odd. Through chess, which I had learned from my father and brother while at primary school, I discovered an alternative social milieu. In autumn 1970, I joined the Sea Mills Chess Club, where my younger brother Robert was a member, and played with him for their 'A' team in Division One of the Bristol and District Chess League. The captain, Ken Derrick, was to become a good friend of mine and we competed together in weekend chess congresses, including the West of England Challengers Championship, held at Easter 1972. Ken secured third place out of eighteen, missing out on joint first place by half a point. I finished in a lowly twelfth place. We eventually came to share similar left-wing views. He worked in the office of Mardon, Son & Hall, printing and packaging manufacturers, in central Bristol, and belonged to the Association of Scientific, Technical and Managerial Staffs (ASTMS) Union, headed by its flamboyant general secretary, (David) Clive Jenkins.

On the global stage, chess was becoming an arena for power politics. In July 1971, at the height of the cold war, a world chess championship match began between Bobby Fischer, of the United States of America (US) and Boris Spassky, of Union of Soviet Socialist Republics (USSR) in Reykjavik, Iceland. During the match I happened to be travelling as a foot passenger on a ferry to France for a short camping holiday with my seventeen-year-old brother Robert and we followed one of the games on the ship's television. Becoming an admirer of Fischer's chess ability, I tracked most of the 20 championship games leading to his eventual triumph. Only later did I come to recognise the hidden scenario of a wider confrontation between the US and the USSR in the cold war.

I was still not at all alert to international politics, which rarely surfaced in conversations at RWP. Startling events within Britain, such as the workers' occupation of the Upper Clyde Shipyards at the end of July, also received little if any attention at work, and even the clerical chapel's problems were not aired openly. In August 1971, only seven months after he had been elected as FoC, Malcolm Howard revealed that he was leaving the works to take up a post at one of RWP's subsidiary companies. His announcement came just a month before the Industrial Relations Bill had received royal assent. In the knowledge that this would most likely be a formality, Howard reported that he felt little could be achieved in pursuing the chapel's policy of insisting that all new employees must enrol with the union, as the Bill set forth the principle that all workers should have the legal right to join or not to join a union.[11]

In September 1971, the chapel elected my colleague and fellow scheduler, 34-year-old Dave Gerrish, to replace Howard as FoC. Many years later, when I interviewed Dave in 2009, I learned that in sharp contrast to my youth of job-hopping, he had started his working life, aged sixteen, on double shift as a spool cutter in the factory.[12] After eighteen months the factory manager, Fred Smith, approached him and suggested that he should transfer to the planning office on day work as a 'runner' because he was "not really suited for working on the shop floor". This proved to be agreeable to Dave who told me:

> I was going down the [Bristol] City ground twice a week for training and playing for junior sides. So, every other week I couldn't go. So, I didn't get picked then if I didn't go down. So, I thought that [the change to day work] would be better for me and I didn't particularly like shift work anyway.[13]

Then, in 1955, aged eighteen, Dave was conscripted into the army for two years under the 1947 National Service Act. Fortunately, this was an experience I never had to go through; the call up (conscription into the armed services) had ended in 1960 when I was thirteen years old. In 1957, Dave was to return to work at RWP as a scheduler for the glue laminating and lacquer machines. Fourteen years later, when he took over the role of FoC of the clerical chapel, he was still working in production control. Before the formation of the chapel, he told me that he had gone "five years without a pay rise".[14] Dave's experience helps to explain why discontent existed.

In November 1971, industrial unrest reached Bristol. A large unofficial stoppage, involving six unions and 6,000 workers, began at Rolls Royce in North Bristol, which was not resolved until 3rd January 1972, when a mass meeting of the workforce voted to accept a pay increase of £1.50 a week. In contrast to RWP where shop stewards had largely kept their distance from politics, in Bristol's aircraft industry there was a strong set of left-wing shop stewards that included both Labour and Communist Party members.

1972

In the early 1970s RWP upped its strategy of investing in the development of new products together with expanding production. Consequently, on 1st January 1972, the company changed its name from the Robinson Waxed Paper Company to RWP Flexible Packaging (RWP FP) to reflect its growing range of complex products. The scope was extraordinary and imaginative, including vacuum packaging for cheese, pouches for food preservation by thermal sterilisation (Sterilite), coated UPVC for blister packaging of pharmaceuticals, and laminated bonded paper/foil coated with heat seal peelable lacquer for the formation of aluminium foil pouches for medical products.

These advances placed additional pressure on the production workforce to cope with increased demand, which in turn required greater support from the administrative and technical staff. This altered the relationships between employers, managers and workers at the company because they had to adapt in order to deal with new problems. The personnel department, for instance, was to become more heavily involved in handling labour relations.

This transition came at a time when class conflict across the country was becoming more and more pervasive. British miners struck work on 9th January 1972, the first national action by the National Union of Mineworkers (NUM) since 1926. Widespread power cuts followed, and the impact of strikes affected people's daily lives. I can remember rushing out to buy candles for lighting the home without feeling animosity towards the miners. Instead, I was very sympathetic to their cause, largely because I could not see myself engaging in such dark, dirty and dangerous work.

I got my news mainly from the television and reading the local press. On the weekend I would leaf through the pages of *The Sunday*

Times because, as well as reporting on current events, such as the impact of the miners' industrial action on Britain's power supply, it had a good chess column. The shock of learning about the abominable killing of thirteen peaceful protest marchers by British troops on 30th January 1972, known later as "Bloody Sunday", is the one distressing event that lodged in my memory.

On 9th February, the labour relations crisis prompted the government to declare a state of emergency and introduce a three-day week to conserve coal supplies. Around one and a quarter of a million workers were laid off; then, just over a week later, the NUM settled for the government offer of a 20% increase, and the three-day week was called off.[15]

Pay was the most urgent concern for the clerical chapel, and indeed for all our factory chapels at this time. This was because inflation, measured by the change in retail prices, had increased from five per cent in January 1971 to almost eight per cent in November. The company had tried to undermine the clerical chapel's attempt to secure a wage increase by tempting members into accepting a job evaluation scheme. The proviso for joining the scheme was that staff must forgo union negotiated pay rates.[16] Non-union personnel had been placed on this scheme, known as "the salary plan", and were thought to have benefitted. It caused a big stir among staff, and a few of our chapel members on higher grade work transferred their allegiance to the Technical, Administrative and Executive (TAE) section of the union because this allowed them to sign up to the scheme, as the TAE did not have a recognition agreement with the company. The clerical chapel officers refused to have any involvement in the plan,[17] and agreed to join the factory unions in a non-cooperation policy with the company because of the lack of progress in local pay negotiations. This policy was not voted upon. At a chapel meeting in January, the members present were simply informed "that the chapel would have to adhere to the policy of non-cooperation".[18]

The national crisis in industrial politics may have been transforming the consciousness of workers in other places, but at the RWP plant in Bristol its impact was variable. Discrepancies were particularly noticeable between white and blue-collar employees. Office managers, unlike their counterparts on the shop floor, *expected* staff to do their bidding. So, despite the non-cooperation policy, they would approach us on a one-to-one basis. Thus, it was difficult for staff to defy a manager's order knowing that this might not only lead to formal disciplinary action, but risked an informal backlash of intimidation, harassment and even victimisation. Consequently, implementing the policy in the offices proved to be difficult and was further hindered by confusion over what 'non-cooperation' actually meant.

Union members in staff areas, including me, found it hard to oppose managers' instructions openly. In self-protection, we tended to suppress any public expression of animosity towards either managers or non-unionists. Many non-union staff shared a similar dread of altercation. This fear of confrontation meant that a tacit, mutual understanding to put differences aside developed between union and non-union staff, which enabled working relationships to be maintained. However, the fear it was based on was undermining. Psychologically it increased a sense of isolation, separation and mistrust. It served only to mask a deepening divide between those who were union members on one side, and managers and non-union staff on the other.

I was becoming aware of the marked contrast between my own work situation and the responses of manual workers in Bristol and beyond. They were showing no such reservations in challenging not simply their employers but the state. I heard from local news reports that in the second week of July 1972, 300 scaffolders in Bristol had come out on strike, which brought construction work in the city to a halt and, most remarkably, by the end of the month tens of thousands had joined them in a series of selective stoppages across the country's building industry.

On 21st July, in a conflict over containerisation, and the removal of dock work outside the jurisdiction of the ports, an injunction was served on seven dockers to stop picketing at the Midland Cold Storage Company. They refused to comply. The court issued warrants for the arrest of five of them for contempt of the National Industrial Relations Court. Later that day, four were detained and sent to Pentonville prison; a fifth joined them after his capture while picketing the prison the following day.

Dubbed the Pentonville five, their imprisonment triggered a huge outcry. Striking NATSOPA printers prevented the publication of London newspapers. Forty thousand dockers, including 1,400 employed at Avonmouth docks, Bristol, and around 130,000 others, stopped work in protest.[19] The strikers disregarded the advice of their national union leaders and openly defied the law. Their action was one of several political strikes that occurred between 1969 and 1972. This was a new phenomenon, for political strikes had been rare before this time. Legislation only served to accentuate the trend. Mass strikes continued until the Pentonville five were suddenly released, just six days after they were first arrested.

This break in the tradition of keeping politics out of trade unions began to have an impact on me. When I watched left wing politicians and union officials on the television news, I came to see that they were rarely represented in a favourable light. Moreover, they were often berated in the national and local press. This led me to question the biased role of the press. At the time Anthony Wedgwood (Tony) Benn had been the MP for the Bristol South East constituency since 1950 and was regularly criticised by the Bristol based *Western Daily Press*. On 24th July 1972, its 'Search Light' editorial derided Benn's defence of the Pentonville five:

> Inflammatory speeches have been made by Labour party chairman Mr Anthony Wedgwood Benn, and by Mrs Barbara Castle.
>
> Mr Benn says that millions in Britain will respect men who would rather go to jail than betray what they believed to be their duty to their fellow workers.
>
> Millions of others will of course, regret that these men should equate duty with defiance of the law.

Despite being critical of the Act, the *Guardian* too was arguing that the Pentonville five's actions should not be defended:

> It is true that the five dockers ought not to have disobeyed the Court. All laws are binding, whether you like them or not. But none of this alters the case against the Act itself. Used as it has been so far the Act is an unstoppable machine for making martyrs.[20]

Both perspectives implied that the dockers were not justified in resisting a law that threatened them and their families' livelihoods. Although relatively new to trade unionism, and short on political awareness, I felt sympathetic to the dockworkers' cause. While employed in the offices of the National Dock Labour Board in 1969, I had learned of the demeaning ritual of registered dockers who, up to 1967, had to present themselves as available for work at the dock gates twice a day (morning and afternoon), to see if they were required. This daily routine, and their constant battle to improve the appalling and dangerous conditions in which they operated, promoted a strong sense of loyalty to each other and their trade union.

I also happened to have had personal contacts on the docks. A former classmate, Richard Hook, who I had known since I was five years old, had worked on the docks in the late 1960s. My father-in-law, Joseph (Fred) Maull, had been employed as a dock labourer since the late 1950s at Avonmouth and, until it closed as a working port in 1975, Bristol City Docks. While he was not an active trade unionist, he nevertheless possessed a deep sense of loyalty towards the Transport and General Workers Union. Like many of his fellow workers, he equated the steward with the union. He trusted his shop steward to do what was best for him and his fellow workers. It was always a source of pride that he had dutifully followed his advice and directives, including taking strike action.

While shop floor union activists at RWP understood the significance of the Industrial Relations Act and the dockers' resistance, this was not necessarily the case for most of RWP's workforce. The majority of its employees lived in the northeast suburbs of Bristol while the dockers, on the whole, lived near Avonmouth docks or the city port. So, as a consequence, no close personal affinity existed between the workforces. This meant the local and national media could fill the void and skew the 'facts' in their commentary on both the dockers' dispute, and the twelve-week national building workers' strike. Indeed, their reports were to become more and more hostile. Ironically, while Bristol dockers received strong backing from the print unions in London, and elsewhere, particularly Liverpool, little support came from the print unions in Bristol itself. I suspect that a contributing factor to this discrepancy was the cohesive impact of community solidarity combined with workplace militancy which still existed in East London and Liverpool.

Thus, while hundreds of thousands of men and women in industries around the country, including Bristol, were swept up in militant industrial action, white-collar staff at RWP were relatively unaffected. Conflict continued to be avoided and the non-cooperation policy did not hold in staff areas. In November 1972, the FoC, Dave Gerrish, openly complained about the poor support he had received from chapel members. He felt that "the chapel's credibility as an organised collection of trade unionists had been weakened."[21] He also said he was not receiving enough help from the full-time officials of the union. Despite these problems, membership of the chapel remained stable in 1972, though attendances at meetings dipped.[22] It was as if members wanted the benefits of belonging to a trade union and the protection it could give in times of trouble, as a kind of insurance, but did not want engagement.

However, even as our FoC was expressing a sense of isolation, several strands of radicalisation were just beginning to converge. Resentment was aroused by the Government's imposition of a three-month pay freeze in an attempt to control inflation, which by then was running at around ten per cent. This, together with rising unemployment, added emotional fuel to the politics of industrial conflict. The increase was from a relatively low base; meaning workers' expectations were higher. Then in December 1972, 160,000 engineering workers and 10,000 dockers struck work in protest against the £50,000 fine imposed on the Amalgamated Union of Engineering Workers (AUEW) by the National Industrial Relations Court.[23] The bitter memory of unemployment during the 1930s was still present in the minds of older workers and they passed it on to some younger union members through families, like those of former clerical chapel secretary, Derek Williams. Once aroused in conflict a resolve never to go backwards took hold.

Amidst all this industrial turmoil, Chris and I had exchanged our two-bed flat in Highridge for a three-bed council house in nearby Withywood. Although by the early 1970s, the 1950s post Second World War council estates of Hartcliffe, Highridge and Withywood, situated on Bristol's southern border, were recognised as being among the most deprived areas of the United Kingdom, our house, which was part of a terrace situated in a quiet cul-de-sac, with a small green in the middle, and close to the local primary school, felt like a haven.

Moving from a flat to a house marked an important transition in our lives. We were intent on the stress and excitement of transferring our belongings to, and settling in, our new home rather than any concerns about politics and industrial unrest. It was a busy and expensive time. The rent, rates and water charges amounted to £6.61 (by the end of 1973 this had increased to £7.70), which was around a third of our income. The newly introduced Access charge card provided us with the credit to buy paint, wallpaper, wardrobes and carpet for our main bedroom.

Not only were we thus in debt, but there was also much work to do, including a front and back garden to maintain.

Relocating to the house in Withywood brought us into a network of working-class families. Chris's sociable personality made it easy for her to integrate into the community. She settled in quickly and went on to make some close friends. I came to know something about the lives of the people on the estate who were friendly enough, though I did not lose that uneasy feeling of remaining somehow an outsider, observing others.

The community we had entered was certainly all working class, but it actually contained considerable variations in family circumstances and types of employment. Next door, on one side of us, lived a couple with two children who had bought their council house some years previously, one of the few properties on the estate that were privately owned. In residence on the other side was a couple with one grown up daughter and one around fifteen years old. The father worked as a motor mechanic foreman, maintaining a small fleet of vehicles for a mushroom farm in Langford, Somerset, about nine miles from our home. His skills helped me to keep my car on the road. The mother was employed at Hales cakes in Clevedon, fifteen miles away, and the firm used to lay on a coach to pick her up, along with many others who lived in the Withywood and Hartcliffe area.

Their immediate neighbours, Joyce and Albert, had four young children. Albert worked on the railways. Looking after two sons and two daughters, all under ten, was a full-time job, which left Joyce, despite being relatively poor, with little option but to be a stay-at-home mum. An older couple lived opposite us whose children had left home. She was a full-time carer for her husband who was blind. Most of the other neighbours were middle aged. One woman worked at the Wills tobacco factory, then in Bedminster. She had a teenage son who, during the evening, enjoyed playing his electronic organ. Her husband was a lorry driver for Holms, Sand & Gravel, whose depot was in Hotwells on the dockside. Though our cul-de-sac was generally calm and orderly, occasionally he would clash with his next-door neighbour, a coach driver, over parking spaces for their 'company' vehicles.

At the time I took the diversity in their lives for granted. But it was through my Withywood neighbours that I came to learn about aspects of Bristol stretching beyond my own background and working life.

Chapter 3

Coming Through: A Learning Process (1973–1975)

1973

Over a year as a production scheduler meant that by the beginning of 1973, I had acquired enough knowledge to be able to mediate conflicts of interest between sales and production with confidence. The running order of jobs would often prove contentious. Settling these required assessing the 'make-ready' time for producing and mounting the stereo rubber printing plates and then working out what impact these were likely to have on the timing of other orders waiting in the pipeline.

All this necessitated a process of negotiation. Thus I would be involved in independent 'parleys' between account executives, who used reasoned arguments in support of prioritising their customers over others, and the production supervisors who understood the labour processes in each specific area. All this diplomatic dealing sometimes resulted in lengthy discussions. As I gained experience, I was able to do this and always strove to be objective. In the end I made the final decision. If the parties concerned were dissatisfied, they had the option of appealing to their senior managers, who of course could, and sometimes did, overrule my judgement.

One particularly argumentative supervisor in the rubber-mounting foundry, Geoff Thompson, used to complain regularly about my priority changes to the scheduling programme. When he got argumentative, he tended to stumble over his words, which prolonged our altercations. Also, he regularly used snuff and conversing with him while he sniffed powder up his nose could be somewhat disconcerting. Regardless of his anachronistic habit and regular protestations, as I got to know him, I came to realise that behind Geoff's front of apparent grumpiness lay a more gentle, humorous man. We never fell out as we developed a real liking for one another and because of this we were always able to resolve our disagreements satisfactorily.

In order to schedule the work, I used to gather information from those who were involved in specific processes. This meant that I formed good relationships with several shop floor workers, particularly NGA printing machine operators and skilled workers in the plate-making foundry where the rubber stereo relief printing plates were mounted on rollers for use on the rotary flexographic presses. I had a planning board, both in the foundry and the flexographic printing office, so that the treble shift supervisors, machine operators and support staff could see the jobs released for printing, the order of priority and what preparatory work had to be done.

I felt at home in the friendly environment of the foundry. Situated away from the noise of the printing presses, the foundry was a place where, besides being able to talk about work activities, it was possible to engage seriously in conversations on social, political and trade union matters. I came to know Geoff Collard, a leading member of the NGA chapel (later to become FoC and then a full-time official), and Jim Cox, the NGA chapel secretary, well. Both Geoff and Jim played a long-standing role in labour-management relations in the firm and were people I would seek out for advice. Geoff was one of a small team producing stereo rubber flexographic printing plates. He was a confident articulate man, if rather brusque at times. In the past he had played football with Dave Gerrish and had sympathised and supported Dave's effort to keep the clerical chapel going. Jim, who worked in the stereo rubber mounting section, was quite different, thoughtful and quiet. But I came to value his opinion on inter-union relations and of labour-management affairs in the company.

I also thought highly of Joe Hall, the NATSOPA machine chapel FoC, though I did not always agree with him. He worked in the wax coating and laminating department, another area that I covered in my scheduling job. Joe had a remarkably equable temperament. Nothing seemed to faze him; he took everything in his stride. A pragmatic and a canny negotiator, backed by a membership some 400 or so strong, Joe spent as much time on union business, as he did working on the shop floor. His members held him in great regard, trusting him to represent their interests, and he was to figure prominently in my involvement in trade unionism.

Most of the union stewards at RWP FP—there were at least three dozen of them, including health and safety representatives—eschewed mixing politics with trade unionism, placing their energies on looking after their members' interests at work. This contrasted with the impact of the Communist Party and Labour Party stewards in the aircraft industry, and in some engineering and manufacturing companies, including printers. At St. Stephen's Press, for instance, the Communist Party had an active factory branch. NATSOPA had two Communists on their Bristol branch committee, William (Bill) Wookerjee of St. Stephen's Press and Harry Dean, who worked at Mardon, Son & Hall.

Left political activists like these contributed more than simply party politics, or even discussion of left ideas. To those they worked with, they communicated possibilities. One example of this occurred in my own family. In the summer of 1973, my younger brother, Robert, who had just left school, was working in a large refrigeration plant at Avonmouth, Bristol where the union representative, a member of the Communist Party, made an important impression on him. Robert told me,

> he was known locally as the "Avon Mouth"... I can't remember his name but his views on politics and society I remember to this day. He was a bit of a stereotype looks wise—Che Guevara beard, beret etc. ... very intelligent and his oratory was really memorable—a real character.
>
> He gave me a lift on the back of his motorbike (no helmets) during work time, back to Portway School to get my A-Level results. He encouraged me to aim for higher education which I had not considered at the time, so I owe him a lot.

Robert would eventually go on in 1977 to work as a scientific research assistant for the NHS in London; in 1979 as a junior laboratory technician at St Mary's Hospital, Portsmouth; and between 1992-2015 he was a section manager for haematology at the Royal Sussex County Hospital, Brighton.

* * *

In April 1973, Chris confirmed that she was pregnant and that our second baby was due in late October. A couple of months later, a few weeks after our summer holiday in Goodrington, Devon, Chris awakened me at around 1.30 in the morning. She had stomach pains and asked me to call a doctor. I was only half conscious and grunted something along the lines that perhaps we should wait a while to see if the pain would pass. Wrong answer! She made it abundantly clear that she was not prepared to suffer any longer! After a wait of two hours or so, the doctor came and after a quick examination, immediately called for an ambulance. On arriving at the hospital, she was diagnosed with acute appendicitis!

I came to visit her early the following morning. She already had her operating cap and gown on ready for surgery. Very calmly she said to me: "It's touch and go Mike". My heart turned over and the blood drained from my face. I thought she was referring to her life! On realising I had misunderstood, she told me that the baby had a 50-50 chance of surviving the operation. A very worrying few hours ensued. However, the operation was a success. Our unborn child was unharmed, and Chris, rather frazzled, came home to convalesce.

* * *

External political and economic circumstances were beginning to impinge on peoples' everyday lives. In August and September London suffered a series of IRA bomb explosions. The Provisional IRA had brought the war to England, which added to the problems of Edward Heath's Conservative government. In early October, the first of three trials began of the 'Shrewsbury 24' flying pickets, charged with conspiracy to intimidate, causing affray and unlawful assembly while attempting to persuade building workers to join the national strike, in September 1972.[24] Also, in early October 1973, the fourth Arab-Israeli (Yom Kippur) war began. The Organisation of Petroleum Exporting Countries (OPEC) raised oil prices by 70 per cent. This had a grave effect on the British economy, and indeed elsewhere in Western Europe and Japan. A period of stagflation followed. Inflation, already historically high, was running at just over nine per cent.

At RWP that autumn my own connections to the union were consolidated. Due to a few resignations, and the departure of the clerical chapel's secretary, Derek Williams, from the company, replacements for the chapel committee had to be found. Dave Gerrish, the FoC, approached me to see if I would stand for the vacancy of secretary. Somewhat apprehensively I agreed. At a poorly attended chapel meeting in October 1973 I was elected as secretary; Roger Vaughan, a wages clerk and a founder member of the chapel, replaced the former chair, Trevor Mildren, who had resigned after being promoted to head the scheduling section. Two new representatives were chosen for the accounts section. However, two vacancies in production control were left without nominees, consequently Dave, the FoC, along with the deputy FoC were left with little choice but to cover these roles.[25]

Dave Gerrish, FoC clerical chapel (1971-74) on the left; Moger Woolley, DRG Group chief executive, in the centre; David Richards, DRG FP managing director, on the right, 1979.

A couple of days later, Dave informed the company that members of the clerical chapel would no longer cooperate with non-union staff, such as withholding information that could have an impact on the efficient running of the business. This attempt to demonstrate that despite losing a few key members the chapel was still prepared to push its agenda of unionising non-managerial staff focused minds. Fred Taylor, NATSOPA full-time Bristol branch secretary, was called in. He struck an agreement with the management at RWP FP that allowed him to meet with all non-union staff in order to tell them about the benefits of the union and invite them to join. His exhortations fell largely on deaf ears.[26]

In the latter part of 1973, I was preoccupied with events at home rather than work. On the evening of 28th October, Chris' contractions quickened, and her waters broke. She was taken into Southmead Hospital. I had stayed at home to look after Amanda, our four-year-old daughter, so I was unable to be present at the birth of our second daughter, Jacqueline (Jacqui), in the early hours of the following morning. However, this did not lessen our joy at what was a particularly poignant occasion, given that we could have lost her when Chris had been rushed to hospital, a few months before, to have her appendix removed.

In early November, while I was on leave, sharing the responsibility with Chris of running the home and caring for our children, the government declared a state of emergency, as miners and power workers took industrial action. On the 18th December the Shrewsbury Pickets, Ken O'Shea, John Carpenter, Des Warren, Ricky Tomlinson, John Llywarch and John McKinsie Jones were all found guilty of affray and unlawful assembly. O'Shea and Carpenter were cleared of "conspiracy to intimidate" charges. However, the following day, the others were found culpable of the conspiracy charges made against them by a majority verdict of ten votes to two. Prison sentences were imposed on Warren, three years, Tomlinson, two years, and Jones, nine months, though Jones was released on appeal. O'Shea and Carpenter received suspended sentences.[27]

1974

Edward Heath, the Conservative Prime Minister, decreed a three-day week from 1st January 1974 on all commercial electricity usage. Special exceptions applied to essential services such as water supply, railways, ports, sewage, refuge disposal and airports, as well as hospitals, producers of medical equipment, chemists, supermarkets and, strangely, newspapers. TV stations had to shut down by 10.30pm. Fortune favoured RWP, which was exempted as it produced packaging for pharmaceutical firms, and therefore fell into the category of companies that manufactured vital materials for wrapping medical products. The company was thus able to work on non-essential products, such as chocolate bar wrappers, as well, and took full advantage of this unexpected opportunity.

Heath intimated that the introduction of the emergency measures, which had led to unscheduled power cuts, had been taken largely as a consequence of the miners' and electricity workers' overtime bans. An external political event was also a significant factor. Daily life was seriously disrupted by the Organization of Arab Petroleum Exporting Countries (OPEC) oil embargo. I can recall long queues at petrol stations, and many restricted the amount of fuel you could purchase because of the shortage.

In the event fuel stocks held out, causing the miners to up their action by announcing that they would strike on 6th February. Heath immediately called a general election. Labour came to power after this 'Who governs Britain' election but was left short of an overall majority.[28]

Three weeks after Harold Wilson had been declared prime minister of a Labour minority government, the clerical chapel faced a crisis. Our FoC, Dave Gerrish resigned; so did his deputy. Despite being on the chapel committee, I had no forewarning of their decision to quit. Losing both of them left a huge gap, not just in the formal structure of the chapel but also in the experience and knowhow within the branch. At a meeting on 26th March, calls for their replacement were met with silence and averted eyes from the remaining 24 attendees, including me. The departure of our union officers raised the question as to whether the chapel had a future.

In the following few days I met with Keith Palmer, the accounts office union representative, to discuss what should be done. He was a young man with a good sense of humour who had shown a strong commitment to maintaining a union voice in the company. We agreed that I would put my name forward as FoC and he would apply to become my deputy. He approached colleagues in his office to see if they would be willing to fill the other vacant positions. Margaret Allen, a young enthusiastic clerical chapel member, who was later to become Mother of the Chapel (MoC), agreed to accept being nominated as secretary. We were all under 30 years old, with relatively little experience and a shared uneasiness about taking on our new roles. On 2nd April, the chapel confirmed the positions for three months (chapel rules at this time required that the FoC and Deputy FoC positions automatically lapsed every quarter, though those holding them would be eligible for reappointment if nominated).[29]

I had taken on a formidable responsibility at a time of volatile labour relations, though ironically I was about to face an unpredictable danger, not through work but on a short holiday. On 12th April, the first day of the Easter break, I set off happily to play chess at the West of England Annual Chess Congress Challengers' Tournament in Torquay. While travelling alone in my old blue Ford Anglia, a lorry I was following threw up a stone, which hit my toughened glass windscreen. It held together but separated into multiple small pieces, completely obscuring my vision. I immediately applied the brakes and punched a hole in it large enough for me to see and pull in safely by the side of the road. I cut my hand in the process. As I did not belong to any motoring organisation such as the AA or RAC, I removed the rest of the glass and completed an uncomfortable and unpleasant journey at speeds between 30 to 40 miles an hour with the wind rushing into the car, through my hair and back out again.

It was Easter and most of the stores were closed. I booked into a hotel and searched the town for a motor accessories shop. Striking lucky I found one open and bought a temporary flexible Perspex windscreen. This I fixed in position by threading it behind the wiper blades and wrapping it around the door support pillars so the ends were inside the car and it remained supported when the two front doors were shut. Considering the stress caused by this accident, I did reasonably well in the chess congress, winning two matches, drawing three and losing one.

I had little time to dwell contentedly on my performance. On my return to work after Easter I faced a far more challenging test. I had inherited a dispute from the previous FoC over a £1 premium productivity/efficiency payment. This had been nominally accepted by RWP FP management, but turned down by the Pay Board, the government agency that controlled prices and wages. This body had been set up by the Heath government to curtail what it deemed as inflationary wage demands and continued to function under the Wilson administration until its abolition in July 1974. As a result, to strike or threaten to strike to force an employer to contravene an order of the Pay Board was still illegal at the time of our claim. Therefore, the union and the company had to demonstrate that the proposed premium supplement to the wage bill had been or would be based on increased productivity.

It was a matter of finding a form of wording that would satisfy the Pay Board. Eventually, the Board gave the go-ahead to pay the shop floor staff, but it withheld permission to pay clerical union employees on the grounds that their claim was dependent on them showing they had taken or would take on increased responsibilities.[30] The clerical chapel committee discussed the Board's conditions on Thursday evening May 16th. By this time the mood had shifted decisively and most remarkably the chapel officers were insistent that the productivity payment should be honoured. They approved the introduction of an immediate overtime ban and sanctioned a 'work to rule' from 3rd June. Regardless of its being illegal, this resolution produced a quick response. On Monday 17th

May, my deputy and I, together with two management representatives, met with a Board spokesman, and this time consent was given, so we cancelled the industrial action.[31]

Despite feeling somewhat out of our depth because of the complexities of the 1973 Counter-inflation Act, we had achieved a positive outcome from our first negotiation with the company. Our triumph was somewhat marred by someone reporting us for leaving the premises directly after our meeting, half an hour before time. This taught me a vital lesson: as a shop steward you have to be aware that you are constantly being monitored.

These engagements took me away from the office. But unlike the shop floor union representatives, in my absence no one was allocated to cover my job. So, this left me playing catch up with my work once these meetings had finished. The area of production scheduling for which I was responsible was not an undertaking that could be handed over at short notice. Before going home, I had to ensure there were enough production orders allotted, with the appropriate documentation, to keep the machines running for at least the next 24 hours. As my first negotiating experience had demonstrated, by not returning to the office before going home, I risked loosening my grip on my scheduling function, giving management, if they so wished, an excuse to move me into less interesting and lower paid employment.

There were several reasons why I did not want this to happen. I liked the logistic challenges I dealt with and valued the significant amount of autonomy I had in my scheduling role, which enabled me to keep control over certain aspects of my work without managerial interference. Moreover, my connection, cooperation and friendships with shop floor workers had become important to me. Our discussions ranged from production problems, frustrations, gripes, bosses, and the state of the business and unions to lighter subjects such as clubs, cars, sport and general banter. Gradually, I was able to overcome the suspicion of factory staff in the printing and waxing departments towards white collar workers. I derived great satisfaction in providing them with 'inside' information on the state of the business, workload and the possibility of overtime working.

As ever I was learning from the people around me, though I soon began to realise that in other ways I was not naturally suited to my new role as FoC. I was aware that I was not good at persuading others. Motivating members was a difficult task for me. I especially disliked having to ask for support from those members with whom I had little active association during my working day. That old sense of being an outsider, with me since childhood, inhibited me from expressing an easy surface of jovial camaraderie.

Temperamentally, I could never overcome a feeling of being on the margins and unable to exert influence, regardless of ostensibly being the FoC. I think this was partly the result of my lack of confidence and a reserve as an individual. But a special social factor was also there. Coming from a working-class background, I often felt awkward with some of the people in the office who I perceived were middle class, such as sales account executives and secretarial staff. Inwardly I held back because I was uncertain how to be with them and doubtful as to how they saw me.

In contrast, I was inclined to have a straightforward attitude when I faced senior management, for I saw them simply as 'the enemy'. This did not mean that I showed antipathy towards them. I suspect that I was able to draw on the ability I had acquired as a boy in hiding my feelings because of my constant fears that my parents would find out that I was being sexually abused. Then I had internalised my sense of shame, now I controlled my feelings of anger.

During those first few months of 1974, the annual negotiations on pay and working conditions entailed a swift learning curve. As a recently elected FoC, the complexities of these agreements and the intricacies involved in presenting annual claims for revisions were new and unknown. I had to comprehend the difficult relations between unions, as well as making myself aware of industrial regulations and employment law, and the conventions that tended to establish the terms of negotiating.

The various print unions each presented their wage petitions to the British Printing Industries Federation (BPIF), which represented the general printing trade employers, including DRG. This decision to negotiate independently was because the NGA wanted to ensure the continuation of traditional percentage differentials between craft and non-craft workers, rather than sharing wage increases equally irrespective of gender or skill, as SOGAT had been demanding. SOGAT prioritised narrowing the gender pay gap in the industry by insisting on the upgrading of women's jobs, by abolishing the Class 4 pay rate, a path not followed by the other print unions. Consequently, the lack of support for SOGAT's radical proposals about the importance of addressing the over representation of women in low paid work, combined with concern about the cost to the print industry, meant the BPIF rejected SOGAT's appeal.

For SOGAT negotiators the improvement in women's pay compared with men's, through the elimination of the Class 4 pay rate, constituted an essential requirement in any settlement. They did, however, indicate a willingness to consider significant concessions on the other parts of their claim. Yet the BPIF, having settled with the NGA, NATSOPA and SLADE (the art and designers union), doggedly refused to concede. Adamant on ending Class 4 and putting the BPIF's offer to ballot, SOGAT advised its members to reject the offer and they did so. The BPIF still would not budge. Consequently, SOGAT called on its members to strike.

As I had only been elected as a FoC in April, I had not been directly involved in NATSOPA's side of the negotiations. Apart from SOGAT, the other print unions had shown little or no commitment to advocating the removal of Class 4 because they had relatively few female or male members on this grade. It happened that women and men in my chapel, and other NATSOPA clerical chapels in Bristol, were linked to Class 2 and 3 rates. Consequently, while the dispute between the BPIF and SOGAT escalated, we were able to raise our women's pay rate as a percentage of men's earning from 90 to 95 per cent.[32]

I was on holiday, when on Monday 10th June, 1,700 SOGAT members, employed at RWP FP and other factories belonging to the DRG group in Bristol and the surrounding area, walked out on strike. A significant minority of these strikers were women. Having settled their pay claims with the BPIF, my union, NATSOPA, along with the NGA, SLADE and the Amalgamated Union of Engineering Workers (AUEW) instructed their members to continue to work normally, and they did so.

On 11th June SOGAT strikers gathered outside the TWGU's office (renamed Tony Benn House in 2012) in Victoria Street, Bristol. They then marched a couple of hundred metres along the road, their numbers holding up the traffic, to the imposing 210-foot-high (64 metres) DRG headquarters on the corner of Victoria and Redcliffe Street to make their feelings felt. The following week SOGAT announced it would call out all 5,000 of its members in the West Country at midnight on Thursday.

The employers and their supporters mounted pressure through the media. Tom Jones-Sandell, secretary of the South Western Printers' Alliance of the BPIF warned that this could lead to company closures.[33]

A DRG spokesperson expressed concern that if the strike continued hospital supplies of syringes and surgeon's gloves could run out for the lack of medical packaging. The Conservative MP, Paul Dean predicted "that the stoppage would affect hospitals within a week."[34]. Soon after I had been elected as FoC a rumour started that Arthur Smith, the FoC of SOGAT's finishing chapel at RWP FP, was a Communist, which turned out to be untrue; because he was marked as a leading advocate of the strike, his detractors wanted to besmirch his name. Communists certainly could exert influence, though only when what they said was in accord with union members' views. They were being turned into all powerful bogeymen simply because of the militant mood among the workforce.

The strike spread to some regional newspapers and threatened to engulf the 'Fleet Street' national press. A defiant SOGAT asked all its members working on national newspapers to come out in support. However, just hours before they were due to down tools, News International, Associated News, Thomson Newspapers and Westminster Press conceded by agreeing to eliminate Class 4 within their provincial operations, thus ensuring that their national newspapers, whose employees were covered by a separate agreement with the Newspaper Publishers' Association (NPA), were not hit. The proprietors of the *Financial Times*, *The Times*, and the *Daily Mirror*, all with provincial newspaper interests, stubbornly held out, and were eventually forced to close when their SOGAT staff stopped work.

Michael Foot, the Employment Minister, stepped in and set up a secret meeting of the two sides. Eighteen hours later they reached an agreement, and the strike was called off. Though the wage increases for men on the higher rates of pay, Classes 1, 2 and 3, were, along with the flat-rate cost-of-living bonus, the same as those first offered in April,[35] SOGAT had achieved one of its key objectives, the abolition of Class 4. As a result, SOGAT's 80,000 women members benefited, while women and low-paid members of the NGA, SLADE and NATSOPA also profited. By the time I came back from holiday the strike was over.

The compromise did leave a continuing difficulty. Craft pay differentials, the difference in wages between workers with diverse skills in the same industry, were to be disturbed by the flat-rate cost-of-living clause. This would become a source of conflict between the NGA, the other print unions and the company, as skilled printers sought to restore their long-established craft differential of 12.5 per cent, after the government's statutory (force of law) income policy was replaced by a voluntary one in 1975.

In late October 1974, two weeks after Labour had won an absolute majority of three in that year's second general election, I resigned as FoC of the clerical chapel. Margaret Allen took over as the Mother of the Chapel (MoC). I accepted the deputy FoC's role. The chapel minutes attribute my decision to stand down to "apathy amongst the Chapel members",[36] and their disconnection from what was happening to and around them, but there were other contributory factors. My personal circumstances had changed. Chris had just begun to work evenings as a cleaner at the Homeopathic Hospital, Cotham Hill, Bristol, which meant her leaving home at around 4.30pm. Thus, I had to rush back home after work to collect the children from our neighbour, Joyce, who had kindly agreed to care for them until I arrived, which was usually between 5.30 and 6.00p.m.

Our five-year-old daughter, Amanda, had just started at the local primary school. As with all children she needed support and encouragement at this crucial stage in her life, which placed additional pressure on our already busy lives. As it happened, Amanda settled in well at school, making many new friends, and Jacqui, now a year old, had already started walking. Having a young family brought great pleasure, though it was not all plain sailing. Money was tight, and as Chris and I were both working we spent little time together and thus were simply unable to fully share in simple pleasures like sitting together talking about our day, watching the TV or listening to music.

Not long afterwards we took in a temporary lodger, Ken Lee. We had met him while we were on holiday in Austria in 1972. He was in the civil service, and after gaining promotion, which required him to move to Bristol, he needed somewhere to stay during the working week, while he looked to buy a house. He lodged with us for a few months over the winter of 1974/75 and, by chance, his presence would have a major impact on my life. One evening, while I was out, he happened to answer the door to a man selling the *Workers Press*, a weekly paper sold by the Trotskyist Workers' Revolutionary Party (WRP), formerly the Socialist Labour League. Ken engaged in a discussion with the caller. When he mentioned this to me, little did I know that in 1975 visits such as this one would become fairly regular.

Margaret Allen, the new clerical chapel MoC, worked in the accounts office, and had a firm grasp of what the unionised white collar staff at RWP Flexible Packaging wanted. She felt that they simply wished to be taken seriously, listened to with respect and treated 'fairly'. I think she understood our members more than I did. But probably she did not realise that to satisfy these desires would have required a fundamental cultural change in management behaviour towards its organised white-collar workers.

RWP's culture of benevolent paternalism towards its white-collar staff can be traced back to the beginning of the twentieth century. The company was reluctant to see this undermined by an outside body, particularly a trade union. Progress took a long time. An early attempt to establish a clerical union at RWP had occurred in the late 1950s, but the company nullified this challenge to its authority by granting managerial status to some senior employees, which entitled them to free lunches and better pay. The call for office staff to unionise had come from a few of these defectors. When the company bought them off junior staff were left without a spokesperson, leaving them more open to management diktat. It would be another six years before white-collar employees secured limited union recognition. Even then the company did not take them really seriously. Bar one or two exceptions, for several years managers at all levels simply continued to act as they had done before.[37]

This legacy had only come under sustained attack from the clerical union in the early 1970s. Yet despite a shift in mood, especially among younger staff, management's power showed a remarkable resilience. I was convinced that in order to change this situation it was crucial to bring staff round to seeing that their interests converged with those of the shop floor workers. This sense of a common identity was vital for acting together to achieve successful outcomes in negotiations with the company. However, its creation had only been partial.

Many shop floor workers distrusted staff believing that they acted as an extended arm of management. Some could recall with bitterness how, during a six-week strike in 1959, clerical staff had been used as 'blacklegs', assisting in the operation of production machines. Nonetheless, the FoC of the machine chapel, Joe Hall, recognised that it would be in his members' interests to advance unionisation in the offices to reduce the chances of strikebreaking in the future.

Really the main obstacle lay with our own members. Ambiguities in the class position of clerical staff sustained the closeness of some clerical workers to management and constantly served to undermine the effectiveness of the clerical union. This inhibited the kind of solidarity that existed among manual workers and reduced any significant pressure on management to alter.

* * *

In January 1975, in order to identify itself with its parent company, RWP Flexible Packaging re-registered as Flexible Packaging (DRG FP), part of the DRG group Ltd. The company issued a new *Handbook for Staff Employees.* It included rules that formed part of the contract of employment. Staff were instructed to certify that they had received the handbook and accepted the rules by signing a detachable slip. Though the handbook confirmed that the company recognised the clerical chapel of NATSOPA as representing its members' interests in the workplace, it neglected to mention that the union was involved in determining pay and dealing with grievances and discipline. This exclusion clearly aimed to diminish the union's role, and some of my work colleagues and I refused to sign this 'contract'. I still have the copy without my signature. This was a small act of defiance, but important nonetheless for our morale.

At our clerical chapel meeting later that month, we decided we must arrest the sense of impotency and disillusionment which was beginning to take hold. We agreed to petition the company for a post-entry closed shop. This meant that union membership would be obligatory a certain time after commencing employment. The advantage of this would be to increase the power and effectiveness of the chapel *vis-à-vis* management. A union with a closed shop agreement like this could impose discipline on recalcitrant members, whose actions were seen as undermining union policy and principles. Ultimately, this threat of disciplinary action was somewhat abstract for the extreme penalty of dismissal was unlikely to be put into effect by the company.

I supported this post-entry closed shop because I believed it would provide us with a real opportunity to reduce the power of management, but I felt that actually attaining it would require pressure from the factory unions. Understandably, they were unwilling to reject working with non-union office staff, unless we could get our members to reciprocate, and we were some way from achieving that.[38] There were other concerns too. One former union colleague of mine observed that the closed shop would lumber us with a group of half hearted "waverers, people who didn't really want to be in the union."[39]

The closed shop proposal was put on hold, though attendees at the March clerical chapel meeting did support a proposal to join with the federated house chapels (group of NATSOPA chapels within DRG FP) in their non-cooperation policy with the company over the delay in updating local agreements. This petered out as the BPIF presented their final offer in the annual pay round, which NATSOPA and SOGAT voted to accept. It was to be paid in two stages, the first in April and the second in November, to comply with the £6 per week (£312 per annum) maximum increase allowed under the 'voluntary' Social Contract agreed between the Trade Union Congress (TUC) and the Labour Government. The NGA, however, gave the offer the thumbs down, and decided to go it alone with an overtime ban.

This sanction began on 5th May. As well as affecting DRG FP, it also hit the provincial papers. The *Bristol Evening Post* was forced to apologise for the reduction in the size of its newspaper due to the action,[40] which continued for seven weeks.[41] The ban did not have such a dramatic effect at DRG FP as orders had already begun to diminish as a recession kicked in. I had difficulty convincing my colleagues on the factory floor that there had been a sharp fall in product demand and that it was not a company ruse to keep unions in check. There seemed to be no end to the years of low or negative growth, which made it so hard to improve conditions simply through union action at the workplace. Consequently, I became open to listening to those advocating alternative socialist policies to address the problems faced by the workers.

In early summer, the WRP again called on me while canvassing the area. No doubt encouraged because our lodger had bought their paper, they were following up their visit in the previous winter. I opened the door to Richard Edwards, a schoolteacher then in the WRP, who had graduated from Southampton University in the late 1960s, and we stood on the doorstep talking for a long time. I found what he had to say challenging and thought provoking at the same time. He put forward the view that trade union militancy alone was not sufficient to defend workers from capitalist exploitation and this struck a chord. He seemed equally convinced that developing a mass revolutionary party was urgently required at this time. I knew nothing about either the WRP or the history of Trotskyism. Nonetheless, Richard's arguments aroused my interest.

I started taking and reading the WRP's professionally produced daily paper, the *Workers Press*. Articles in it alerted me to the possibility of change and awakened in me a thirst for knowledge about the building of a socialist movement. However, I eschewed making any commitment, despite pressure to do so. Naturally cautious and reserved, I felt uneasy about signing up to an organisation that I knew so little about. While I was very interested, I was not prepared to devote myself to a cause of which I was unsure, moreover one that could impinge on my personal life. I had already relinquished my role as FoC in favour of the deputy FoC position in an attempt to free up some time to be with Chris and the children.

In early July, Margaret, the clerical chapel MoC, announced that she would stand down at the next quarterly meeting. This was a blow. She was popular and had gained great respect, especially from her colleagues in the accounts office, other MoCs in the factory and from the NATSOPA Bristol branch, of which she was a committee member. In September, rather reluctantly I stepped in again to fill the void. John Nicholls, who had only recently been taken on as an accounts clerk, filled the deputy FoC's position. He was in his late twenties and had a lot of nervous energy to expend, which fuelled his enthusiasm. However, he did not always think before he spoke, a habit that would sometimes get him into trouble.

Within days of taking up my union role as FoC, Ken Shipton, the production control manager, called me into his office and said that if I continued with my union activities there would be consequences, inferring that he could make life difficult for me. I immediately raised an objection to Shipton's menacing remarks to the personnel manager, Clive Oliver, and asked the NATSOPA full-time Bristol district secretary, Fred Taylor, to take up my case. Officially his protest had the desired effect, but other than a quiet word no action was taken against Shipton. While clerical chapel members in my office often complained to me about Shipton's personal bullying behaviour, they were not prepared to make a stand against him, reflecting the weak union culture among the company's white-collar staff. I found it disorienting moving between this vacillating environment and the long-established forthright union culture on the shop floor. I knew where I felt more comfortable.

*   *   *

Throughout 1974 and 1975, I somehow contrived to combine all this intense union involvement with my passion for chess, which constituted a deep source of fulfilment for me. In 1974 I had competed in a five-round tournament, which included a draw with a young Susan Caldwell, who went on to become a very good player as well as a member of the Socialist Workers Party. In 1975 I played in two weekend congresses. In early January, I scored a respectable three points out of six in the amateur section of the first Welsh Open Chess Championships at Cardiff. At the Cotswold Chess Congress in late May, I only managed to win two games out of six. I always hoped to do better in these tournaments; though I rarely achieved more than a 50% success rate, my interest in the game never flagged. I gained such immense pleasure simply from playing. I learned too from chess; I came to recognise when to trust my intuition and developed the ability to think logically. Chess became my obsession and no doubt Chris thought she had become a chess player's widow.

Looking back, I can see that my absorption in pursuing what interested me, whether chess or trade unionism, did not take into account the impact it must have had on Chris. Although I did look after the children most evenings when Chris was at work, I was increasingly preoccupied. This was to be even more marked when I became further involved in revolutionary politics.

* * *

Over the course of 1975, progressively I gave my evenings over to digesting WRP's economic and political analyses of the crisis Britain had experienced in the first half of the 1970s. I was committed to defending jobs and fighting for higher wages and better working conditions. I agreed with them too in wanting to replace capitalism with socialism, but I remained at a loss at how this could be achieved. I decided I needed to develop my understanding of how the capitalist economy worked and why the WRP believed that this was a period ripe for a world socialist revolution. The WRP, in contrast, appeared utterly convinced they had the answer to how to bring down the capitalist state.

Someone in the British ruling class took them seriously as a threat to law and order for, in September 1975, the Special Branch, along with around 100 police, raided the WRP's College of Marxist Education in Derbyshire, expecting to find an arms cache hidden in the grounds. They had been apparently tipped off by reporters from the *Observer* newspaper. The premises were subjected to a six-hour search and nine ·22 bullets were found in a cupboard and taken away, along with a few documents. No one was arrested or charged. The following day the *Observer* published an article saying that WRP members had hinted weapons were buried in the grounds and that they had gained access to secret cabinet minutes. It also included the claim of the actor, Irene Gorst, that she had been held and interrogated at the Marxist Education College for several hours against her will.[42] Six plaintiffs from the WRP, including its former general secretary, Gerry Healy and the actors Corin and Vanessa Redgrave, sued the *Observer* for libel. It would be three years before the case would be heard.

The general view on the left was that the bullets had been planted. I had no reason to believe otherwise. The WRP, in its paper, *the Workers Press*, and in public statements, had repeatedly said that it completely opposed acts of terrorism. Instead of discouraging me, the whole bizarre affair of the raid, the publicity and the legal case, only fuelled the feeling that rebellion was once again in the air, and that perhaps I should put aside my reticence and join the WRP in the fight for socialism.

In the same month as the raid, September 1975, the first of four episodes of *Days of Hope*, written by Jim Allen, produced by Tony Garnett and directed by Ken Loach, was shown on the BBC, though Garnett had to fight very hard to get it on. The series was to have a profound effect on me. Its depiction of individuals' lives moved through the industrial and political life of the working class from 1916 to 1926, including the 1921 miners' lockout and the 1926 General Strike. It illustrated, in a dramatic form, the merciless treatment of conscientious objectors in the First World War, the brutality of the soldiers deployed by the British state in the Irish war of Independence, and the shenanigans of the trade union leaders and high-ranking labour politicians in 1921, 1924 and 1926. However, it was seeing how the consciousness of one of the leading characters, Ben, changed because of what he experienced, that made the deepest impression upon me. Initially, Ben willingly enlists in the army during the war. He then serves in Ireland in 1919-20 and deserts as a result of having witnessed the abusive and violent treatment of innocent people there. Finally, he ends up joining the Communist Party and speaks with certainty and confidence.

Jim Allen's own personal insights as a working-class socialist writer made the script memorable. After leaving the army in 1947 he had worked as a building labourer, a docker and a miner. Surprisingly, given that Allen had been a member of the WRP's forerunner, the Socialist Labour League, and both Garnett and Loach had spoken on WRP's platforms, the *Workers' Press* did not carry a review.

Engaging with this realistic historical drama and the WRP's theoretical writing made me acutely aware of needing to understand the world I lived and worked in. This startling new recognition resulted in me becoming dissatisfied with dealing with the practical everyday demands of union work. I wanted an absolute answer on how to overthrow capitalism and replace it with socialism. Very few people in the office seemed remotely sympathetic towards such a quest, but I found one ally in Bob Brain, who had recently joined the company as a sales account executive. His father worked on the factory floor in the ink-mixing room. While a student at Ealing Technical College, Bob had studied French and Spanish. He was a member of the Labour Party and he, too, was searching for answers about how to change society for the better. Later, we would form an effective partnership in turning the clerical chapel into a real force, as office workers faced the threat of the introduction of new technology.

While I was being propelled towards root and branch transformation, in contrast fears about job security were permeating the minds of staff, both in the offices and on the shop floor. Amidst the recession, and the subsequent fall in new orders, we were forced onto the defensive. Our clerical chapel approved a motion stipulating that in the event of staff reductions, only voluntary redundancies would be accepted.

Then in October a dispute broke out on the shop floor between the NGA and DRG FP over crew numbers when a printer, under instruction from his FoC, refused a temporary transfer to another job. He was suspended and the whole of the NGA chapel walked out in support. The matter was quickly settled in house as the company conceded and the suspended employee was reinstated. This was an important victory, as the company were searching for ways to reduce the numbers employed.

The NGA chapel's success in forcing the company to back down reflected the unity, confidence and strength of its members. Yet this demonstration of rank-and-file resolve was regarded as a threat to the constitutional procedures of the decision-making machinery of the union at branch and national level. The NGA Bristol branch committee censored the FoC and the chapel for not involving them in this dispute because it concerned staffing levels, which could have had implications for members working for other companies.[43] Only the local branch had the authority to alter labour agreements.

Other Bristol workers too were fighting against the impact of the recession. For example, in November, 630 workers struck work at the Avonmouth works of Commonwealth Smelting Ltd, a subsidiary of Rio Tinto Zinc, for its refusal to go through the normal negotiating procedures in a dispute over redundancies and pay cuts. The dispute, which received massive publicity, was to last seventeen weeks before the company relented and the strike was called off.[44]

Around this time DRG FP restructured the scheduling functions. This altered my job. I retained responsibility for the flexographic machines, lost the wax coaters and wax laminators but assumed the planning role for the lacquer laminating machines. One small though significant part of my new brief was to monitor a 50-50 agreement between the NGA and NATSOPA on the manufacture of grid lacquer coated paper, a product that offered heat sealing qualities for the packaging of medical products such as syringe needles. Because an etched cylinder was used, grid lacquering could be produced on both lacquer machines, run by NATSOPA operators, and gravure print presses, staffed by the NGA, though the latter were far less efficient. Concerned about the falling print orders, the NGA managed to push the company into giving them a half share of this work, which was increasing in demand. My responsibility was to make this operational and supply regular updates on the amount produced by each 'partner'.

I relished this job because it required me to liaise with the union representatives of the NGA and NATSOPA as well as the machine operatives concerned. The discussions about how to proceed strategically were exactly the aspects of my role in production scheduling which engaged my interest and enthusiasm.

Chapter 4

Only One Shade of Red (1976–1977)

1976

By the start of the year orders at DRG FP were beginning to show signs of picking up as the country slowly started to pull out of recession. I believed this was a favourable time to announce I was stepping down as FoC. When Margaret resigned, I had taken on this role out of duty, rather than willingly, because no one else was prepared to put his or her name forward. I had the experience. In January the clerical chapel elected John Nicholls, who had been my deputy since September, to take over from me. I was relieved that we had an energetic and enthusiastic young person from the accounts office with a more abrasive style in his dealings with management than I had. I took a back seat by filling the production control representative spot rather than putting my name forward for the deputy position to give John more space. Also, I really needed the opportunity to gather my thoughts about the way a more equal society could be achieved. Jim O'Brien, who worked in the despatch office, took the post of deputy FoC.

John's first task was to address members' complaints about being overburdened with extra work. During the recession DRG FP had reduced staffing levels in the office through voluntary redundancy and natural wastage. This had resulted in an increased workload for many of the remaining white-collar staff. They were expected to work more flexibly, and some were forced to accept temporary job transfers to share out heavy workloads. This was stressful and a handful of members, including a few working with me in the production control office, reported that the stress was having a detrimental impact on their health.

Frustrated by management's failure to respond to the clerical chapel's request to start recruiting once again, especially as the factory had started working overtime to deal with the increase in orders, the full-time union official was called in. In March, he approached the company and made the case for taking on six new office staff. The company dragged its feet so the clerical chapel vetoed overtime.

Despite no longer being the FoC, I was still suggesting plans of action. On 19th May, an emergency chapel meeting approved my proposal to step up the pressure by refusing to handle any extra work generated by overtime working in the factory. However, only half of the members were present and although the motion was carried by 23 votes to twelve this only represented around one third of the total membership. The management tested the chapel's resolve by threatening to suspend anyone who refused to work 'normally'. They held out one lifeline; if the inflow of orders continued at their present rate then recruitment of up to five out of the six clerical posts we had requested could go ahead. On this basis the chapel committee retreated and lifted all the sanctions it had imposed.

Conflict ensued because some chapel members portrayed this episode as a humiliating climb down by chapel officials. While John Nicholls was competent and keen, he could be brusque and dismissive and alienated some members. The chair of the clerical chapel, Roger Vaughan, resigned his position in protest saying that "as soon as we had to stand up and be counted, we failed."[45] The underlying problem was that in reality the chapel committee had a weak mandate because my resolution to escalate industrial action had been passed at a poorly attended meeting. Moreover, it was difficult to put into effect because managers and non-union staff could cover some of our work. I found the whole episode extremely disheartening. It accentuated a growing suspicion I had that it was not possible to bring about real changes in the power dynamics in work and employment relationships without the support of a political party on the left.

* * *

During 1976, my contact with Richard Edwards of the WRP became more frequent. In May, just over a month after James Callaghan had been installed as Prime Minster, following the surprise resignation of Harold Wilson, the WRP replaced the *Workers Press* with a new daily paper, the *News Line*. It too was professionally designed, using the latest technology, computer typesetting and web-offset printing, but I missed the more analytic content in the *Workers Press*. *News Line* was more descriptive and polemical and adopted a more popular tabloid form, including a sports section with horse racing tips.

However, I continued buying my copy from Richard. He delivered the paper to my home daily, collecting the money I owed each week. I did not think about this at the time, but I must have been regarded as a 'trade union' contact. After much persuasion from Richard, I finally

Christine, Jacqueline, Michael & Amanda Richardson, 1976.

accepted an invitation to a south Bristol party branch meeting on a Sunday at a local pub in Withywood. When I arrived, nobody was there. Within a few minutes, however, Richard pulled up on his motorbike accompanied by a youngish woman, riding pillion. We entered the pub, which was virtually empty, and Richard spoke to the landlord. We were directed to the lounge and I sat facing him across a long wooden table, on which he placed a well-thumbed book and some papers. The three of us turned out to be the meeting!

All I can recall from this strange occasion is that Richard, speaking like a schoolteacher, began his opening address by reading something from the works of Leon Trotsky. I listened in concentrated silence and left feeling bemused. I realised an extant south Bristol branch of WRP did not actually exist and this tiny gathering was an attempt to get one off the ground. Despite this rather bizarre initiation to revolutionary politics, I continued my association with the WRP through Richard.

* * *

Chess and daily life filled the long hot summer of 1976. In the last weekend of June, I played in the Bristol Open Chess Championship along with my friend and Sea Mills chess captain, Ken Derrick. In the fourth round my opponent was Anne Sunnucks, three-times British Women's Chess Champion. After 67 moves she came out the winner. I later discovered she was a major in the Women's Royal Army Corps!

Three weeks later, Chris and I took the children on holiday to Rockley Sands, near Poole in Dorset. Like thousands of other working-class families that glorious summer, we stayed in a caravan for a fortnight. The good weather allowed us to spend most of our time outdoors with visits to Poole pottery, Bournemouth and Sandbanks, where you could not walk barefoot because the sand was so hot. These annual holidays were extremely important for both Chris and me. We really needed time away from the stresses and strains of work to relax. It was our one chance to enjoy an extended period of being together as a family.

I missed the July clerical chapel meeting where my political ally, Bob Brain, was elected as chair to replace Roger Vaughan. The chapel deliberated over a proposal from the FoC, John Nicholls, for a jointly run job evaluation scheme. Members unanimously rejected the idea, because not enough was known about how it would work. They asked John to go back to management to find out the detail,[46] which suggested to me it had been initiated by them. John did, however, deliver some good news. Our petition to increase staff numbers in the clerical areas by six had not been in vain, despite our retreat from taking industrial action. The company had finally agreed to recruit five school leavers to ease the intensified workloads.

As elsewhere, union members in Bristol were becoming increasingly unhappy with the tight rein on pay under the Social Contract. The decline in real wages and increased unemployment had resulted in protests and demonstrations opposing pay restraint across the country. The local unemployment rate in Bristol had risen alarmingly over the last year, from three per cent in August 1974 to over six and a half per cent in August 1976.[47] Our members were uneasy and restless.

In September, it came to light that some non-union clerical staff had received higher pay increases than unionised staff, by an average of two and a half per cent. The chapel demanded parity, but the company refused. In protest, a paper ballot of clerical chapel members authorised, by a large majority, the imposition of sanctions on holiday and sickness cover. The factory unions backed our action at first but withdrew its support after the intervention of the managing director, Moger Woolley.[48] He claimed that the limits of phase two of the Social Contract had prevented the company from paying *unionised* staff more than the £6 maximum. Woolley insinuated that non-union staff were not bound by the 'voluntary' contract made between the TUC and the Labour Government. I could not see how this could be so. Why could it be legitimate to give preferential treatment to non-union members? No justification was offered.

After the factory chapels withdrew their assistance, the clerical chapel met to assess the situation. The majority of members were in no mood to give up. I put forward a three-pronged strategy to progress our claim. First, I proposed that we lift all the sanctions that were due to begin on the following Monday, 8th October; second, that management be approached to form a committee of four with equal representation from the union and the company, and a chair appointed by the Department of Employment, to seek a settlement of the dispute. My third proposal was the sting in the tail; we should submit a revision of the clerical agreement to read that "all clerical staff [should be] members of the union." This meant in practice a closed shop.[49]

All three proposals were passed unanimously. After much prevarication the company did agree to meet the NATSOPA district secretary, Fred Taylor, and the Advisory, Conciliation and Arbitration Service (ACAS), a non-departmental public body of the Government, at the end of January to discuss our claim for pay parity with non-union staff and the closed shop. The company had misjudged the mood of our members, yet it further antagonised the chapel by installing a computer terminal in the accounts office without proper consultation with union representatives. In response the clerical chapel supported my proposal to refuse to cooperate with its introduction unless the company accepted a guarantee that staffing levels would not be reduced, and those operating the terminal would receive extra pay after training.[50] But at this stage I had not fully realised the significant organisational and process changes computerisation could bring, as well as how susceptible jobs would be after their introduction.

* * *

In the meantime, Richard Edwards, who I had come to like, invited me along to another WRP meeting to try and establish a viable branch in south Bristol. This time several people were present at the Plough Inn, near Parson Street railway station, Bedminster. The subject of a series of expulsions from the party came up. I was completely ignorant why these had occurred. But on learning that Alan Thornett, a shop steward who had a strong following at the Morris Motors car plant in Cowley, Oxford was among them I expressed concern about the irrationality of infighting saying I thought we should be focusing on how to combat capitalism.

My high-minded intervention was met by an awkward silence. At the time, I was unaware of the schismatic history of Trotskyism. Nor had I had any experience of the intolerance shown by the WRP to those who deviated from, or challenged, what had been established as Party orthodoxy. I had no previous knowledge of or involvement with far left politics but I felt decidedly uncomfortable with the imperious message I was getting, either you are with us or you are against us.

Much later, I found out that from the end of the 1960s until his removal, Thornett had played a key part in developing a 100 strong WRP branch in Oxford. He had also contributed to expanding branches in the western region, which in total, including Bristol, had about 500 members.[51] Nearly half of these had been expelled from the WRP along with Thornett. Then in December 1974, Thornett, with around 100 former WRP members, formed the Workers' Socialist League (WSL) in opposition to the leadership of the WRP by Gerry Healy. They regarded him as not only authoritarian but as subordinating the interests of working-class members, like those Thornett represented at Cowley, to a doctrinaire style of politics.

I was thrashing around in the dark and felt unable to articulate my thoughts. Yet, I was still propelled to find out more and put this confusion down to needing to learn more about Marxism and Trotskyism. I joined the WRP.

1977

With a twinge of guilt about my love of the game, my year started with yet another chess tournament. I wondered what the Russian revolutionaries would have said. I suspected that the general secretary of the WRP, Gerry Healy, certainly would not have approved. But I found an ally in Tom White, an Oxford member of WRP Western Region, who welcomed me into the fold as a fellow chess player and told me of Lenin's love of the game. He was a Cowley full-time deputy senior shop steward who had been close to Thornett, though he stayed loyal to the WRP during the internecine factional struggle in 1974. After the mass expulsions, WRP's influence in the Cowley motor works was considerably diminished and Tom White was left to rebuild WRP's membership in the plant. In the few times I saw him he was careful never to mention this conflict, which must have been personally painful for him.

* * *

On 27th January, NATSOPA's district secretary, Fred Taylor, convened with DRG FP management under the auspices of the Advisory, Conciliation and Arbitration Service (ACAS) to discuss the clerical chapel's petition for a closed shop agreement. Reaching this stage was a significant step forward for the chapel. The sense of injustice, which followed the company's rejection of their recent claim of pay parity with non-union staff, confirmed the chapel's realisation that we needed a closed shop if we were to back up our demands. However, Fred Taylor advised us to modify our claim and press for a post-entry closed shop. This meant that only new employees would be required to join the union. The chapel conceded, but approved that my proposal, for an immediate return to free collective bargaining, should be placed before the half yearly NATSOPA Bristol and District branch delegate meeting in March.[52]

Although the company did not completely rule out our claim, it stated that it would not entertain any kind of closed shop agreement unless a ballot of union and non-union staff was taken in the 'relevant' areas. They also insisted that nothing less than an 80% majority decision would be accepted. The result was a deadlock, though a further audience with ACAS was arranged for 15th February.

* * *

On the evening of 15th March 1977, around 500 NATSOPA delegates from unionised print and packaging companies gathered noisily at Transport House (now known as Tony Benn House) in Victoria Street and took their seats in the upstairs hall, which had a stage large enough to accommodate the Bristol branch committee members.

The DRG FP clerical chapel used a combination of a rota system and volunteers to send the required numbers to its union half yearly district branch meetings. NATSOPA's rules stipulated that at least a quarter of the membership of each chapel had to attend as delegates to these representative assemblies. This ensured that significant numbers of the rank-and-file participated in the union's democratic forums. Their presence was essential to the development of relevant policies to meet changing situations, though in practice radical political motions from below rarely got a hearing.

It was an imposing meeting and connected our chapel to others in Bristol. Three of the nine branch committee members on the top table worked at DRG FP, Margaret Hill (née Allen), former MoC of the clerical chapel, Joe Hall, machine chapel FoC and Doug Gingell, ink and roller chapel FoC. Bill Wookerjee, the branch chair, presided. He was active in the Communist Party factory branch at St. Stephen's Press. Among the other members of the committee were another Communist Party stalwart, Harry Dean, an employee of Mardon, Son & Hall, and Bristol United Press employee, and Labour councillor, Maurice Rea.

I had prepared a text to read in support of my motion calling for a return to free collective bargaining. Relieved to have my chapel colleague, Bob Brain, sitting next to me in support, I nervously waited for my cue. I had never spoken in front of so many people before and I worried that my voice would not carry. I felt so self-conscious that when my turn came, I stood up and began to read out my speech nervously. My voice started to quake; I took a deep breath, and I gained my composure. I argued that the Social Contract had become a one-sided deal. Though I relied heavily on polemics, I finished putting my case with solid evidence:

> Look at the government's record since the introduction of the Social Contract. It has been a one-sided bargain only. I don't have to tell you which side has kept the bargain. Just look at the record.
>
> (1) Rising unemployment, one and a half million which probably has a direct effect on five million men, women and children.
>
> (2) Inflation/rising prices seventeen per cent. It proves one thing; it can't be wages that are a direct cause of inflation.
>
> (3) Cuts in public spending, National Health and Education.

Need I go on? I ask you to reject this Social Contract and make an immediate return to free collective bargaining.[53]

Harry Dean then spoke on the motion from the platform. His position on the Social Contract was somewhat unclear. It seemed on balance he was still critically supportive of it, maybe reflecting the Communist Party's divisions over whether to continue backing the pact between the TUC and the Labour government at this particular juncture. In contrast, the delegates were in no doubt. The vast majority raised their hands in support of the motion.

This result came as no surprise. Unemployment had continued to rise, living standards were falling and there was little evidence of socialist planning. By this time growing discontent among the rank-and-file against the Labour government's incomes policy had already forced the hand of some union leaders, including the president of the Yorkshire miners, Arthur Scargill, the president of the National Union of Mineworkers (NUM), Joe Gormley, and Transport and General Workers Union general secretary elect, Moss Evans, to call for the shackles of pay restraint to be removed.

When these union meetings closed, usually around 40 delegates would pop over to the Shakespeare Inn, just across the road from Transport House. This had developed into somewhat of a tradition over the years. The chance to mix with fellow workers, from other printing and packaging firms across Bristol had proved to be quite popular. By far the most numerous were not members of left groups but non-aligned leftists, in an atmosphere free from the formalities of the union meeting. Some would swap stories about their work experiences, while a few others, like me, would huddle in a dimly lit corner and discuss the evening's proceedings and debates.

Barely a week later, the Labour administration was to form the so-called Lib-Lab pact, a coalition led by Callaghan in order to avoid calling a general election when the country was going through a severe economic crisis. It was a highly controversial move. Neither the Parliamentary Party nor the National Executive Committee had been consulted, though Callaghan had the support of the TUC-Labour Party Liaison Committee. While the 'Left' in general agreed that this pact was made so the government could push ahead with phase three of the Social Contract without the full consent of its party, they differed over how workers should resist both industrially and politically. The International

Marxist Group (IMG), for instance, advocated a one-day national strike against the Social Contract. The WRP, however, favoured a General Strike to bring down the government and adopted the slogan 'Labour to power on a socialist programme'.

While the resistance to the Social Contract was growing exponentially, the important, if somewhat less 'exciting' union organising struggle at DRG FP continued. On 20th May, Fred Taylor, NATSOPA Bristol district secretary, and Joe Hall, FoC of the NATSOPA machine chapel, were called upon to update the chapel on its claim for a closed shop, which I had instigated the previous October. They reported that each of the three meetings they had held with the company, under the auspices of ACAS, had ended in stalemate and said that if the clerical chapel gave its full support, the National Executive Committee (NEC) would declare that it was in an official dispute with the company. By a large show of hands, the chapel confirmed its backing for any action called for by the NEC to further its claim.

This was a real advance. For even if the ten absentees, four on holiday, four on sick leave, and three abstentions were taken as negative votes, 56% of the total chapel membership had voted in favour, knowing the demand might well require them to take industrial action.[54] They were prepared to take a risk.

That summer, Dave Gerrish, the former FoC of the clerical chapel, was promoted to head the scheduling section, and resigned from the chapel. Two recently recruited graduates were assigned to production control, one to programme the polythene extruders, and the other put to work planning the slitters. Both had science-based degrees, and both happened to be members of the Labour Party. They were personally cooperative in their work relationships and friendly in everyday social communication. Yet both refused to join the clerical chapel.

I got on very well with one in particular and had many conversations with him over why he would not join. It was to no avail. He remained an avid supporter of the Social Contract, and deplored confrontation, such as the clash with the police at the Grunwick picket on 11th July when thousands of demonstrators arrived at a national day of action in support of the Grunwick workers, who had been on strike for union recognition for several months. He later secured a position in the company's research laboratory as a technologist and section leader. He would eventually leave the company in 1989. He continued, however, to be active in the Labour Party.

In contrast I was moving in the opposite direction. I came round to the view held by the WRP that Labour governments always betrayed the working class and that the Callaghan Lib-Lab coalition government needed to be brought down.

*   *   *

One weekend in the summer I took the family on a day trip to Oxford in our second-hand Morris saloon car, to show my children where my mother was born and raised. While we were there, we dropped in to see her younger brother, Jim Whitbread, and his wife, Margery, who I had not seen since Chris and I married in 1967. As a child they had been my favourite uncle and aunt, and in the late 1950s had bought me my first watch as a Christmas present. Our visit took them by surprise, but they invited us in and made us feel very welcome, providing jelly and ice cream for Amanda and Jacqui and tea and biscuits for Chris and me.

Jim, and his son Anthony, worked at the Cowley body plant (formerly Pressed Steel). Expecting to find an ally, I broached the subject of the growing management offensive in the car industry. They were tearing up existing union-company agreements, destroying traditional job controls and rationalising production. Uncle Jim's response took me back. He angrily blamed "bloody left-wingers" in the union for the bitter industrial relations climate of the 1970s believing the conflicts would only lead to the demise of the Cowley plant. I concluded that the failure of multiple strikes and disputes over decades to radically improve the lot of car workers had left its mark; somewhat embarrassed, I fell quiet and did not pursue the matter.

Back we went to Bristol in our old Morris car. I would learn later of an ironic antecedent. In the 1890s, Jim's grandfather on his mother's side, my great grandfather, James Dubber, had owned a bicycle shop in St Giles, Oxford. An apprentice working for him, called William Richard Morris, became dissatisfied over his wages, and in 1893 left to start his own business, a bicycle repair shop. In 1913 he established his own company Morris Motors, Cowley, Oxford. By the 1920s it had become Europe's biggest carmaker.

*   *   *

Towards the end of the summer, after talks between Owen O'Brien, the NATSOPA general secretary and key directors of the DRG group, an offer of a partial post-entry closed shop materialised. Given that the clerical chapel had the backing of the NATSOPA executive council, I think the company were concerned that the dispute would escalate to include all NATSOPA members employed by DRG FP. It was an important gain for us.

About the same time as these negotiations were taking place, I agreed to take on the 'revolutionary' task of distributing *News Line* to followers in Bristol South, mostly in the Hartcliffe and Withywood areas. Every morning, on my way to work, I would call into the Red Star office at Temple Meads railway station to pick up my allocation of papers. This was not easy, since often they had not been collected from the platform on which they had been deposited from the London train. Too long a delay would have made me late for work, so sometimes I would simply go into the station, seek out the papers and bring them up to the Red Star office. This did not make me at all popular with the railway staff, but it did mean I could get to work in good time.

Delivery of the papers, except for the odd sale in my workplace, had to wait until I arrived home in the evening. On the weekends I called on subscribers to collect any money owing. The revolution remained notably restricted for the numbers taking the WRP publication fluctuated between 15 and 20. I was meant to encourage them to get involved in the WRP's events, and generally get them to say what they thought about the paper. I was not proactive. I tended only to respond to the few who talked to me. I loathed pressurising people. I was a diligent deliverer of the *News Line* but not very good at rounding up people for the WRP's somewhat infrequent activities.

By early September, negotiations between NATSOPA's full-time officials and the personnel manager responsible for all of DRG's subsidiary companies had produced a draft post-entry closed shop agreement. The agreement was limited to departments where union membership had established a 75% majority. Initially, the accounts office, buying office, switchboard and post section qualified for inclusion, which meant that new recruits in these areas would have to join NATSOPA.[55] If and when other departments attained 75% membership the chapel could apply for an extension to the agreement. At its September meeting, the clerical chapel voted to accept the offer with a few minor provisos. We had achieved a hard-fought gain.

That autumn personal tragedy broke through the 'them and us' battles at DRG FP. Managers, staff and factory employees were united in shock in hearing that our production control manager, Ken Shipton, had lost two daughters in an enormous explosion and fire that destroyed the Raj Restaurant in Stapleton Road, Bristol and the flats above. Later it came to light that Muhammad Arshad, the restaurant owner, was in debt and started a fire in order to make a fraudulent insurance claim for damages. The plan went horribly wrong and all six occupants living in the rooms upstairs, including Ken's daughters, died. Regardless of differences in the workplace we could all identify personally with such a terrible loss.

In Bristol, workplace conflicts persisted and within DRG FP inter-union divisions surfaced, which played into company's hands. The proud craft-based union, the NGA, scuppered the attempt of the other unions to submit a joint union pay claim to the company for in-house extras by taking a sectionalist stance and going it alone. After a few weeks, negotiations between the NGA chapel and DRG FP management broke down over productivity payments and, in the fourth week of November, NGA members walked out in pursuit of their claim. A picket line was established at the works entrance complete with a brazier to keep them warm. I used to stop by daily to talk to NGA officials and pickets who assured me that they did not require the clerical chapel or the other print chapels to strike, because they were confident that the company would eventually be forced to concede.

The directors took the decision to pay full wages to all its employees not involved in the strike, even if as a result of the stoppage they would have no work to do. By going it alone the NGA had given the company this opportunity to drive a wedge between the unions that served to further accentuate the divisions that already existed. With help from both their competitors and customers, management seemed prepared to sit out the strike rather than agree to the NGA's demands. But the NGA chapel was well prepared. It had official backing. Therefore, its members received relatively high strike pay from the union, which enabled it to sustain a long dispute. This fostered close relationships between the national union and its members involved in industrial action.

NATSOPA and SOGAT agreed not to do the jobs of the NGA, or work with non-union labour on any printing machines. But, they argued, it was up to the NGA to prevent printed material from being brought in from outside sources to be further processed in the factory.

The NGA viewed this as strike breaking.[56] Unofficially, I used to inform the NGA officers whenever I discovered that the company had managed to get printed material through the picket lines unseen, because my role involved monitoring partly processed work awaiting the next stage of production. But many orders were outsourced to other firms and did not come through our production control system. The NGA strike would continue into the New Year.

*   *   *

Through the 1970s trade unionists like me had been hearing and reading in the media about union leaders recklessly starting politically motivated strikes. It was true there were union leaders, like Jack Jones of the Transport and General Workers Union and Hugh Scanlon of the AUEW, who were 'left' labour supporters. But their presence was less significant than the feelings among rank-and-file trade unionists. Partly in response to inflation but also, less perceptibly, due to a mood change, young workers were not willing to be deferential and could no longer be intimidated.

Moreover, public sector workers, especially those who were relatively low paid, were becoming aware of the human value of their work, and among them were firefighters. During 1976-77, the rank-and-file members of the Fire Brigades Union (FBU) had substantially increased the pressure on its executive for wage parity with the skilled industrial workforce, plus extra money for the dangers they faced in doing their job. This resulted in the union submitting a pay claim for a 30% increase and a reduction in working hours. The government rejected their claim, standing firmly behind its ten per cent wage increase limit, imposed under phase three of the Social Contract. Despite facing opposition from their own leadership, firefighters reluctantly voted to strike. Three weeks after the Raj restaurant disaster in Bristol, firefighters, who would have risked their lives to deal with the blaze, joined 30,000 of their comrades in the first national strike in the 60-year history of the FBU.

Morally I felt that they deserved the increase in pay they were asking for because of their professionalism and skill, and the courage they demonstrated in attending to emergencies. Firefighters had held back so long. Rightly, in my view, they were tired of risking their own lives while waiting on past promises on pay, which had failed to materialise. I was deeply impressed that they had the resolve to go against the recommendation of their leadership and face the hostility of the government and some elements of the media. I wanted them to succeed in breaking the ten per cent wage increase limit.

Initially their cause received tacit support from some labour politicians, including Bristol MPs, Tony Benn and Ron Thomas. The general public greatly appreciated the work of firefighters and a majority thought that they should be paid more than the ten per cent limit. But while these signs of support were appreciated, they were not enough. The strike began as a pay dispute but quickly turned into a political one because the government would not allow a settlement with the FBU, or any other union, to contravene its incomes policy.

The WRP covered the conflict in the *News Line* by printing a daily diary of the experiences of the striking firefighters in their own words. This was a far more graphic form of journalism than the usual analyses by leading WRP members, and I used to read them avidly. The WRP was arguing that in order to win the firefighters would have to bring down Callaghan's government.

By the end of November, it had become increasingly clear that success hinged on the FBU gaining the support of the TUC General Council. The turning point in the dispute came when in early December the TUC's Finance and General Purposes Committee threw its weight behind the government, advising the FBU to accept the offer of an immediate ten per cent and the phasing-in of a pay formula. The government explained that if agreed this pay formula would be linked to the average earnings of skilled industrial workers, to be implemented in two stages, the first in November 1978 and the second twelve months later.[57]

The FBU wanted the TUC's decision rescinded, and this demand was raised at the full TUC General Council on 21st December. But the TUC reaffirmed its position not to back the strike, which by then had begun to lose public support.

Chapter 5

In and Out the Red House (1978–1980)

1978

After talks behind the scenes, at a recall conference on 12th January, FBU members took their executive's advice and voted three to one to call off the strike. They returned to work on 16th January ending their clash with the Labour Government through a controversial peace formula. *News Line* quoted the London region representative of the FBU as saying that faced with a choice "between the Labour government and the firemen" they had chosen to keep Labour in power at all costs.[58]

The WRP's analysis was that the strike provided the militant firefighters with a socialist consciousness. I sensed, however, that the majority of firefighters were simply struggling for what they thought they deserved, wage parity with skilled industrial workers. The strikers were angry at repeatedly being snubbed and had lost faith in the TUC and the Labour government alike. I believed that the nature of the dispute remained largely an economic one though, no doubt, a feeling of lack of respect for all the work they did was also important. While the WRP was right that some firefighters had been politicised—Terry Kelly, for instance, the secretary of the Crewe FBU, would become a WRP candidate in the 1979 general election—I did not see much evidence of this in Bristol.[59]

Immediately after the settlement, Richard Edwards asked me to drop off a small bundle of *News Line* a few times a week at Speedwell fire station in Bristol, where he said WRP had a 'sleeping' member who would distribute the papers. So, I just left the papers at the fire station reception while I was on my way to work. Whoever the contact was remained 'asleep' and I ceased the delivery. An ingrained pessimistic scepticism stayed with me despite being drawn to the clarity and certainty of the revolutionary politics of the WRP.

* * *

Meanwhile, at my workplace, the post-entry closed shop agreement between the clerical chapel and DRG FP had come into force in the accounts office, the buying office, the switchboard and the post section. Other areas, including my own, production control, were not covered by the agreement. We would have required union coverage to reach the three-quarter mark before we could be included. But only three of the five schedulers were union members—the two graduates employed the previous year remained non-union. In early January a University of Bristol graduate, Richard Johnson, joined the production team to work on a trial project to computerise the forward planning (estimating delivery dates) of orders received, as opposed to day to day scheduling.

As a union representative, I was introduced to Richard within a day or so of his arrival. Much to my surprise I recognised him and he me. We had encountered one another through playing chess. He had been in the University of Bristol's chess team and we had played each other on a couple of occasions. We had a long conversation, in which I asked him to join the clerical chapel. He signed up and told me how his university studies had touched on Marxism. I was intrigued to hear from him that the ex-University chess players had formed a club of their own called Grendel, named after a character described in the early medieval Anglo-Saxon poem *Beowulf.* I would eventually join this club.

Just over a month later Richard received a written warning about his work performance from the manager, Ken Shipton, containing a threat of dismissal. Because I had been subjected to Shipton's scare tactics over my union representative role, I saw this as intimidation and asked the then deputy FoC, Brian Brown, to raise Richard's case with the NATSOPA Bristol branch secretary. The impact was dramatic. In March Richard received a letter from Shipton "rescinding the [written] warning given" the previous month and wishing him "every success for the future".[60]

Shipton had a nasty habit of going for people he regarded as vulnerable. Later in the year I represented a new employee, June Barnard, who had received a verbal warning from him. Along with her supervisor and Brian Brown, we met in Shipton's office. In response to his assertion about her slow progress, she challenged his assessment of her work. He reacted expressing surprise at her "bitchiness" after all the help the company had given her. When I intervened he immediately withdrew his remark. She broke down in tears and the meeting was put on hold. I put in a complaint to the personnel manager and eventually the matter was formally settled. Within the collective memory banks of the chapel, however, it was not forgotten.[61]

* * *

The NGA's printers' dispute at DRG FP, which had started in late November 1977, continued until mid-March 1978 when, after fifteen weeks, the company suddenly succumbed and offered the NGA chapel significant concessions.[62] Craft printers still retained their power. Those confident pickets who had told me that they would win proved to be right. This had been a costly strike for the company. The profits of DRG FP's parent company, DRG, fell in the first half of 1978. In a press statement in May, its chair, John Camm, said that the Holding Company's poor performance was largely due to damaging industrial disputes at DRG FP, Bristol, and in Scotland, the effects of which had seeped into the third quarter of the year.[63] This did not stop the group from making a £10,000 donation to the British United Industrialists[64] who, as well as discretely channelling money to the Conservative Party, also funded the Economic League, which was notorious for compiling blacklists of leftists and trade unionists.

Every year, NATSOPA would circulate a request for chapels to submit the items for consideration at the annual review of the National pay and conditions agreement between the printing unions and the British Printing Industries Federation (BPIF). Referring submissions was a slow formal process, which would begin at chapel level. If approved, these would be passed to the district branch committee to be scrutinised, and if agreed they would then be placed before the National Executive Council. Despite the banal and boring aspects of such a bureaucratic process, it did give members a voice. So, I maintained that the chapel should take full advantage of the process.

Thus, at the May clerical chapel meeting I proposed "Any agreement should assure an automatic rise in wages in relation to the increase in the price of consumer goods, i.e., rate of inflation." I also argued for a reduction in the working week to 30 hours, with the average wage of every worker to remain the same as it was under the old working week. My aim was for wages to follow the movement of prices, while working a shorter week would mean work could be divided to include some of the unemployed.

Brian Brown, the deputy FoC, proposed an addendum, stating that "Retirement age to be brought down to 60 years." This was included in my final motion and was approved with just two members voting against.[65] Our motion was then sent to the Bristol branch. Its response was that as other chapels and branches had submitted similar motions, our aspirations had already been covered. Unsurprisingly, these basic reforms were never met. Frustrated, I turned my attention to the WRP's arguments on the need to acquire a deeper understanding of the class struggle.

* * *

Under pressure from the central committee, Richard, the WRP organiser in Bristol, was meant to send one member from his branch to the WRP's College of Marxist Education near Parwich in Derbyshire on a week's summer course. He persuaded me to register for a week in June 1978. When the time came, I had some last-minute doubts about the wisdom of my decision to go. Though I wanted to learn more about Marxism, I found it difficult to justify to Chris that this warranted a week of my holiday entitlement out of the four weeks plus statutory public holidays I was allowed. She never openly complained but to her it must have seemed incomprehensible.

Another reason for my hesitation was that though I had now become a member of the WRP, I did not feel entirely comfortable; nor was I ever totally committed. I always had reservations. While I had attended the occasional meeting and done some of the donkeywork, like the collecting and delivering *News Line*, I rarely did paper sales or canvassed door to door for new supporters. I had only ever participated in one or two pub sales, which I hated. However, now for the first time I had made a solid commitment and I did not want to deal with the inevitable guilt I would feel if I were to break an undertaking. Putting an end to my uncertainty, I paid the £20 for my board and lodging for the week and set off for Derbyshire in my second-hand lime green Skoda coupé.

I arrived in the recently acquired Skoda at the education college, which was situated in a remote rural area, a few miles from Parwich village. The college, a former country house, with large grounds, was big enough to accommodate 60 students, as well as a small resident colony of bats. Their presence served to enhance the sense of remoteness. As only sixteen students were there that week, the place felt somewhat strange and mysterious. My initial feeling was of foreboding, but I had no one to share this with.

I joined the other students in the afternoon for a preliminary meeting. Apart from a couple of lecturers, we learned that we had to muck in with the preparation of food, cleaning and other chores in between our lectures and seminars. It was explained that the allocation of these tasks would be decided along cooperative socialist democratic lines. It turned out that as I was the only person with a car, by default I had the early morning job of driving to Derby railway station to pick up the education centre's allocation of *News Line*. On the way back my task was to call into the local village to pick up provisions such as flour, bread and so forth. The locals were very helpful and friendly, light heartedly referring to the WRP education centre as the 'Red House'.

During the day and early evening, I helped in the kitchen under the supervision of one of the full-time women WRP members, who were responsible for the cooking and cleaning. I recall opening pear-shaped tins of very salty ham and cutting the contents into small pieces to mix with pasta. Though the woman in charge of the kitchen was reassuring and the atmosphere of the place was relaxed, I remained uneasy. I felt dislocated and out of my depth.

A full-time lecturer at the college, Peter Jones, led our first session. He opened his talk by painting a utopian picture of what living could be like under socialism, where the necessities of life could be produced in abundance and a significant portion of them would be free of charge. He then went on to discuss Marx's *Capital Volume One*. While we were not expected to read Marx, in our stay at the college we were told to buy a copy of Lenin's work *The State and Revolution* at 25p and we read and analysed it in groups of twos and threes over a couple of days. Significance was also given to *Trotsky's Writings on Britain* and we were told how important it was for Marxists to scrutinise the seventeenth century English revolution. The reference to history interested me and I bought a copy, along with Engels' *Dialectics of Nature* while I was there. His chapter, 'The Part Played by Labour in the Transition from Ape to Man' intrigued me, though I was deeply puzzled by the ones tackling scientific problems relating to mathematical calculations, physics and biology.

I was asked to drive a woman staff member to Coventry to call on what WRP described as 'latent' members. One young working-class couple seemed fairly relaxed about our visit but showed no signs of wanting to take an active role in political work. However, one woman, who had recently recovered from a nervous breakdown, was far from pleased to see us. Our visit clearly unsettled her, and I felt uneasy again. The trip made me realise that no extant branch existed in Coventry at this time. I began to wonder whether there were actually many operational branches outside of London.

My experience at the Red House left me confused. But members of the WRP warned against falling into the trap of 'subjective' thinking. They reiterated that one cannot go by 'appearances', because these failed to register that the freedom of the working class can only be advanced by recognising the historical necessity of overthrowing capitalism which was collapsing under its own contradictions. I was told that only the WRP could bring genuine class consciousness among the workers as this had to come from without.

I was bemused by these circular arguments, which were presented as incontestable. I had no means of addressing them critically but struggled nonetheless. I kept dipping into the Marxist literature I had acquired, going through and reflecting on Engels' *Dialectics of Nature*. Searching for actuality beyond one's own personal experience took me into a series of abstractions, which in truth I could not fully comprehend. I could not resolve in my own mind how to integrate subjective and objective perspectives. They seemed to me irreconcilable. I became exceedingly troubled trying to make sense of all this.

On the Thursday, when I was pushed by WRP staff to stay another week, it aroused a state of panic and triggered an overwhelming desire to return home the next day rather than staying until Saturday. When I was questioned why, I just said I was required at home. As it happened a woman on the staff needed to go to Birmingham and so it was agreed that I leave with her in the morning and drop her there on my way home.

I felt relief to be leaving; I suspected that she too was escaping. We were both in good spirits and I enjoyed her company. Just before she got out of the car she said "it was like we were running away together to get married" which made me smile but left me puzzled.

It was so good to get home. A few weeks later I went with Chris and the children on a well-needed holiday to Tenby for six days. The contrast with my discomfort at the Marxist Education College was extreme. We stayed in a flat. We had never been to Pembrokeshire before and we spent time exploring its history, taking strolls along Tenby harbourside as well as relaxing on the beach. Yet I was aware that thousands of workers and their families could not afford a holiday and that they faced another pay ceiling of five per cent, at a time when living standards were falling. An unremorseful Callaghan ignored advice, even from moderate union leaders, that this latest phase of the government's incomes policy would be impracticable and counterproductive.[66]

On my return from holiday, I attended a WRP branch meeting in central Bristol and agreed to go as a delegate to an All Trades Union Alliance (ATUA) convention on the 'Armed Forces and the Trade Unions' at the Wembley Conference Centre on 17th September. Because of the focus on trade unions, the clerical chapel committee agreed to sponsor my attendance, granting me £20 for expenses from chapel funds.[67] The ATUA acted as a front organisation for the WRP, providing a more effective way of reaching large numbers of workers.

The WRP organised exceedingly impressive large-scale dramatic gatherings. Over 2,000 people were there, some in a personal capacity, others, like me, as trade union delegates. The conference focused on the increasing use of the British armed forces as strike breakers—against the firefighters, the air traffic controllers and the naval dockyard workers on the Clyde, where men had blacked working on the Polaris submarine HMS Revenge to intensify their industrial action in support of their pay claim. They were locked out and Naval military personnel were used to load the submarine.

Speakers at the conference also referred to the joint operations involving the troops and armed police at London's Heathrow airport after the Heath government had declared a State of Emergency at the end of December 1973, as well as the more recent arrest and prosecution of Crispin Aubrey, John Berry and Duncan Campbell under Section 2 of the Official Secrets Act and the subsequent trial which had opened at the Old Baily on 5th September in 1978. The atmosphere was electric, and I was carried along by the fervour as 2,000 voices were raised singing *The Internationale* and the tremors of a shared discontent radiated through the hall.[68]

* * *

Callaghan's Labour government faced a setback. On 23rd September, 16,000 Ford car workers walked out in protest against its management's insistence on adhering to the government's unofficial five per cent pay limit. By 25th September, the number of strikers had more than tripled as 57,000 workers brought the company to a standstill.[69] Under the threat of government sanctions should the Ford management concede to the union's demand, the company held firm. The strike, which involved three parties, the Ford Motor Company, the government and the Transport and General Workers' Union, was solid when the decision-making body of the Labour party, its annual conference, began on Sunday 1st October.

Delegates at the conference rejected the Callaghan government's increasingly unpopular incomes policy, favouring in effect the complete abandonment of wage restraint. But the Prime Minister made it abundantly clear that he was not tied by the conference decision and was determined to keep a lid on inflationary pay demands by sticking to the policy.[70] The conference vote reflected the immense pressure coming from below, as demonstrated by the Ford strike. This stoppage was to last nine weeks when, on the advice of their union, Ford workers accepted the company's offer of 17 per cent to settle the dispute. Their success had repercussions for the government as it opened the door for other workers to follow.

The strike was still in progress when, on 24th October 1978, the WRP libel action, taken out against the *Observer* in 1975, came to court and was widely reported. The paper had published an article with the headline "Vanessa [Redgrave] and the Red House Mystery" with the strap line "Girl's ordeal in Trotskyist Hideout". The plaintiffs were the director of the Marxist Education College, Roy Battersby, former WRP general secretary, Gerry Healy, actors Michael Harrigan, Corin Redgrave and his sister Vanessa Redgrave, and the playwright Roger Smith. The trial lasted thirteen days.

The jury unanimously found that the *Observer* had indeed libelled the six plaintiffs by accusing them of hiding firearms at the Education Centre, which was untrue. However, though the accusation of holding the actress, Irene Gorst, against her will was not proven, a technicality in the framing of the question put to the jury resulted in the court concluding that the article as a whole did not "materially injure the reputation of the plaintiffs".[71] The litigants were therefore ordered to pay the cost of the trial of around £70,000. To me at the time this seemed to be a complete travesty of justice.

Not long after, Richard Edwards left the WRP. He had accumulated a lot of debt as a result of carrying out the work of the Party; phone calls, travel and making up the shortfall in payments for the branch quota of *News Line*. His departure triggered a visit to my home by Mike Banda, the general secretary of the WRP and, a short while after, Roy Battersby the director of the Marxist Education College. Both were looking to me to keep the paper round going in south Bristol and to give them names and addresses of members. There were no members, only people who took the paper, though Banda had been given a contact of one ex-soldier who lived in one of the blocks of high-rise flats in Hartcliffe and had subscribed to taking *News Line* on a regular basis. They were civil but left me in no doubt that they were searching for someone to pick up the mantle left by Richard's exodus. I made it clear that I would not take this role on. We parted on reasonable terms. In fact, I gave Roy Battersby a beginner's chess book he had spotted in my bookcase to take home for his son.

* * *

At work, injustice and unreasonableness were exasperating clerical chapel members, who were becoming impatient over the lack of progress concerning their outstanding claim of pay parity with the non-union staff who, on the whole, had received higher pay awards in 1976 than union members. The company stuck to its argument that the continuation of the government's incomes policy had tied their hands. For our part we suspected this to be a cover for discriminating against union members. Management did, however, offer a pay increase of two and a half per cent if the chapel would agree to a reduction in staff numbers through natural wastage. They argued that this would qualify as a self-financing productivity deal and therefore would not breach the government's 5% pay limit. The chapel committee rejected the offer on the grounds that it was the company's responsibility to finance this payment and not the chapel. Ours was just one example of the widespread disdain shown by many workers nationally towards companies hiding behind what had become a discredited incomes policy.

A more worrying development came to light in November. Without consulting with the chapel, the company planned to introduce a change in its system of determining the costs of its products. Immediately, the chapel committee expressed concern about the impact this would have on the work of estimators whose task was to calculate production costs by analysing labour, material, and time requirements.

We soon learned that it was the tip of something of far greater consequence. The company intended to re-estimate and process thousands of orders through a computer. At the time this was a truly startling development. Our response was defensive. The chapel committee argued that the extra workload should be done through overtime only and that estimating jobs should be upgraded. We were utterly unaware of the long-term impact that computerisation of clerical work was going to have on jobs and working conditions.

1979

The New Year opened with a national strike over pay in the road haulage industry. This was the second major dispute in what was to become known as the 'Winter of Discontent'.[72] Pickets were mounted at "road haulage companies, docks, container bases, rail terminals, wholesale markets, warehouses, cold stores, supermarkets and roads."[73] While this did not extend to manufacturing companies such as DRG FP, deliveries of raw materials such as paper, film, foil and inks to the company were disrupted. I recall our manager, Ken Shipton, frantically running around finding ways of getting supplies through and pressurising material control staff to help. Whenever a lorry arrived, a group of senior managers would rush to the window in feverish anticipation.

By the end of January, the haulage strike had all but finished in Bristol, with a settlement agreement of around fifteen per cent reached by arbitration, though not before over one and a quarter million public sector employees had taken part in a Day of Action, on 22nd January, in a protest against their low pay. Anger was boiling over against the impact of the government's incomes policy on undervalued and poorly paid people. Ambulance workers, refuse collectors, gravediggers, nurses, porters, caretakers and others struck work, sending a loud message to the Labour government that they were no longer prepared to put up with poverty wages. Some Labour MPs responded by demonstrating their support. Bristol North West Labour MP, Ron Thomas, took up the case of low earners, asking Shirley Williams, Secretary of State for Education and Science, what she was doing about the "appalling wage levels of caretakers and ancillary staff in our schools".[74]

Less perceptively these major strikes also had an impact on the resolve of active trade unionists like me. In the clerical chapel at DRG FP we set about building the chapel's strength in numbers. These were increasing, partly quickened by the post-entry closed shop agreement, and this boosted our confidence. Three of us in particular —chair of the chapel, Bob Brain, the Health and Safety representative, Ron Rich, and me—were constantly in dialogue, informing one another of ways to advance union influence. I used to give Ron a lift to work every morning and our conversations ranged from office politics to world affairs. Ron was about 20 years older than Bob and me and was a member of the Campaign for Nuclear Disarmament (CND). He had lived in Australia as a British emigrant but returned to the UK after his son was born. He worked in the same office as me on the material control section. His demeanour was much like that of Tony Benn, calm and thoughtful, and he smoked a pipe.

We were hopeful that the clerical chapel would become a proactive body, in order to create a sustainable and effective counterweight against managerial authority over administrative staff. Despite our mood of optimism, we were aware that some members within the chapel were unhappy. They consisted largely of relatively new recruits compelled to join as a condition of employment under the post-entry closed shop agreement. A union directive issued by NATSOPA National Executive Council (NEC) initiated a hostile response from these dissidents who vented their feelings against what they saw as an abuse of union control over its members.

On 1st January, an 18p a week levy was imposed on the whole membership to support 600 workers dismissed by Times Newspapers for failing to sign a new unfavourable contract, the old one having expired. Our chapel committee felt uneasy because paying the levy had been made mandatory rather than voluntary, but we recognised the seriousness of the situation and agreed it warranted a united demonstration of solidarity. Nonetheless, several chapel members complained, angry because they worked in a closed shop area and thus had no option but to pay the levy, since union subscriptions were normally collected directly from members' wages at source. We arranged, therefore, for the area representatives to collect the levy directly from individual members, giving them the opportunity either to raise their objections or show their support.

I met with eight protesters who had strongly and persistently contested having to pay. They argued that the dispute at Times Newspapers had nothing to do with them. One of them was a young woman whose fiancé was an NGA printer who worked in the factory. She had attended just one of the previous six chapel meetings.[75] I explained to her, and the others, the importance of solidarity and how our chapel may require similar help in the future. Though unconvinced, they eventually complied.

This small and seemingly minor episode nonetheless revealed a problem associated with the closed shop agreement. Some members, who had been brought into the chapel through this agreement, felt aggrieved that their union had the authority to discipline them. They became disconnected, and rarely attended meetings or participated in other union democratic processes, such as ballots. *The Times* levy was eventually suspended on 2nd April, just a few days after the Conservatives had won a no confidence vote in Callaghan's government, triggering a general election.

The Annual General Meeting (AGM) of the clerical chapel was due to take place on 1st May, two days before the country went to the polls. In the preceding months, some chapel members, particularly the estimators, had expressed unease at the attitude of the FoC in dealing with their concerns. By this time, Bob Brain and I had developed a close alliance. We had great respect for one another even though we did not always agree. Bob was shrewd, a good listener, and an effective communicator. We sensed that chapel members were looking for a change in the leadership so we decided that at the AGM Bob should stand against John for the FoC office and I would run for the deputy FoC position.

The turnout of 33 for the AGM, though less than 50% of the membership, was slightly higher than the attendance for the 1978 AGM. There were three nominations for the FoC's position, the current holder John Nicholls, his deputy Brian Brown, and Bob Brain, who won comfortably with 20 votes. John then put his hat in the ring for the deputy position but lost out to me by nineteen votes to thirteen. I nominated Brian for the production control representative vacancy because of his experience and enthusiasm for promoting the benefits of belonging to a trade union. We had our differences. He was a devout Royalist and an active organiser in his local church scout group who loathed my 'communist' views, but I believed that it would have been detrimental to lose his organisational skills and guile in representing clerical chapel members. He was elected unopposed.

While, on behalf of the chapel, I thanked John for the work he had done over his three years as FoC, he became embittered and voluntarily left the company at the end of October. I understand now how he must have felt. Fortunately, he was able to secure a position at the union's Bristol branch office as a financial clerk.

* * *

Although I had increasingly immersed myself in union work, I was still convinced of the need for wider social change and managed to find a little time to help the WRP during the general election. Rather than calling for critical support for Labour like other left groups, the WRP had decided it would contest 60 seats in the May election, dismissing the argument that the preservation of workers' jobs and living conditions depended on returning a Labour government under a more progressive socialist leadership.[76] The WRP saw the election as an opportunity to parade its revolutionary credentials in combination with a recruitment drive. Because they were standing 60 candidates the WRP qualified for a television broadcast, dourly delivered by the left-wing actor, Corin Redgrave. They were also entitled to the free delivery of one promotional leaflet, via Royal Mail, to every eligible elector on the relevant electoral registers.

Linda Cheek, the daughter of a popular and principled left-wing union representative for the bus branch of the TGWU, was selected as the WRP candidate for South Bristol. She was committed to socialism and had youthful vigour. I accompanied her to the Bristol City Council offices to register her candidature with the returning officer; we arrived just before 4pm on the deadline day for registration with a completed set of nomination forms together with a deposit of £150. An altercation broke out between Linda and the returning officer, when he wrongly indicated that she was too late to register. After an exchange of some very strong words Linda's registration was begrudgingly accepted.

The election campaign was run from a vacant shop in West Street, Bedminster, near to the DRG Packaging Bags' factory in Argos Road. Posters were placed in the windows promoting Linda as the WRP candidate. Marxist and Trotskyist literature were displayed inside the shop on wooden trestle tables. I, along with other WRP supporters, addressed envelopes in a kitchen at the rear of the building and stuffed them with election material. Concerned about security, the election agent, Mike Driver, stayed at the premises overnight, sleeping in the upstairs bedroom. He was a volatile person to work with and prone to angry outbursts. One morning during the campaign he accidently dropped a full bottle of milk on the pavement outside the election premises. It shattered to pieces, spilling its contents across the path. Angrily he demanded that one of the campaign team clear it up which prompted an almighty row.

Driver also showed little understanding of the pressures other people were under. In his short time in Bristol, he continually pestered me to get more involved in the work of the Bristol branch, slating me for being too heavily involved in my union. When I rebuffed his remarks, he rolled out the mantra that only by building a mass revolutionary party, under the leadership of the WRP, can the working class overthrow the capitalist system and take power. I was of course aware of the failures of the Labour Party but could not see much evidence of mass support for the WRP or indeed any other revolutionary group. I thought his observations were trite and his manner arrogant. Yet I still hung on to the hope that pressure from below would bring about a radically new and better form of socialist organisation.

Unsurprisingly, given Labour's poor record in office and the rise in unemployment from just over half a million to one and a quarter million, the Tories romped home in the 3rd May general election. In Bristol, Labour lost one seat out of the four that they had held since the October 1974 election. In Bristol North West, the Tories defeated Ron Thomas, dubbed "Red Ron" by the media, by nearly 5,000 votes. In Bristol South, Michael Cocks, a Labour right winger, retained his seat with an 11,000 majority over the Conservatives; Linda Cheek, despite being a good and highly principled WRP candidate, came last with 135 votes, 257 votes behind the National Front candidate! Even though Tony Benn held his Bristol South East seat his majority was much reduced. And Arthur Palmer, Labour/Co-op, kept his place in parliament by holding the Bristol North East constituency. Prospects for revolutionary or even radical change looked very grim indeed.

More than ever, I turned my attention to trade union work because I now felt that was where we could have an immediate and real impact. I believed that the battle between the interests of labour and capital within the workplace should be prioritised, even though sometimes this could be tedious and unexciting. I did not sever my association with revolutionary Marxist politics because I remained sympathetic to the theoretical arguments. But the WRP's disregard for the practicalities of trade union resistance left me with a sense of powerlessness. I stepped back from any deeper organisational involvement and confined myself to attending occasional meetings. I also began to read more widely, the literary works of D. H. Lawrence, George Orwell and John Steinbeck for instance, as well as Marx and Engels.

* * *

On 21st May, chapel members gathered again to vote on the national pay agreement, and a new higher grade for the estimators. The 55 present overwhelmingly agreed to accept the terms offered on pay and grading, which finally settled the estimators' grievance over the monetary recognition of the new skills they had acquired to do their work.

We faced a more confident management after the Tory victory in the general election. Unperturbed, Bob and I adopted a proactive approach in representing our members' interests. The first major task we undertook was to draw up a new draft clerical agreement. In our proposal to management, as a priority we included a disputes procedure containing a status quo clause insisting that in the event of any difference between the parties, current practice would not be changed until the disputes procedure had been exhausted or a settlement reached.

Management prevaricated over this. They seemed more intent on establishing a works council in which, as chapel officers, Bob and I were invited to participate, along with the factory chapel FoCs and their deputies. This we declined because the company would not agree to restrict the representation of non-union staff to departmental managers only. We had recently put in a claim to extend our post-entry closed shop to include more staff areas, and to condone non-union representation on a works council would have undermined our ability to recruit these people.

In June, a non-union senior member of staff working in production control left the company. We were informed that he would not be replaced. Applying the status quo clause we had included in the disputes procedure, we told the company that chapel members would not accept extra work arising from his departure. The stand taken by the unionised schedulers not to take on any of his duties forced the company to reverse its decision. It also triggered a response to the draft disputes procedure we had submitted.

Instead of maintenance of the status quo, the company proposed the inclusion of a consultation clause in our house agreement. The general principle was that management would not alter a chapel member's contract without consulting the individual concerned together with their area representative. Any changes affecting a group of members would require the authorisation of the FoC. This was not as strong as the status quo clause we had wished for, but we thought that in the short term this compromise was acceptable.

Bob had spoken with me about approaching the company to see if it would consider adopting a jointly run job evaluation scheme. In

1976, the previous FoC, John Nicholls, had shown an interest in such a scheme but did not provide the chapel with any details on how it would work. Bob wanted us to design a system that evaluated the job content, rather than the job holder, using two assessors from management and two from the clerical chapel. He made the distinction clear because I was against participating in any form of work evaluation because I envisioned the boundaries would blur. Thus, we would end up with a foot in the management camp and have to enforce the results on our members. Inevitably some would lose out. I saw this as a disagreeable prospect, but I suspect most people just assumed it would not be them. The chapel committee thought job evaluation was worth pursuing and, when the details were outlined at a chapel meeting, members voted for us to proceed on the basis that when the assessments had been completed the proposed job grading changes would be referred back for their approval.

* * *

My mounting trade union work had not only affected my part in preparing for the 'revolution', but it was also endangering my beloved chess playing, though I did compete in the Stroud chess congress in the spring bank holiday. That July, I was elected to the NATSOPA Bristol and district branch committee, replacing Margaret Hill who left DRG FP at the end of June. I was one of the ten, including the branch secretary, Fred Taylor, who met at least once a month at the union's office overlooking Telephone Avenue in the centre of Bristol. Four other DRG Bristol employees were on the committee, Joe Hall from flexible packaging, Len White, cartons and printing, and Mike Vine and Stan Maggs, Malago Bags. We dealt with branch administration and organisation, applications for small grants to members suffering financial hardship, donations to groups such as the National Council for Civil Liberties and the Socialist Medical Association, and the rare but onerous task of disciplinary hearings of members brought before the committee over allegedly breaking union rules. At Christmas time we distributed parcels of groceries to our retired members, and a £2 voucher to spend at any Co-operative store.

The Bristol branch committee selected me as one of its delegates to the Bristol Trades Union Council, and Bob Brain was approved as the NATSOPA delegate to the General Council of the Bristol North

East Labour Party. This was the constituency that Ron Thomas had represented between 1974-79, before he lost his seat in the election. Bob persuaded me, in the late summer, to attend a series of talks on the role of planning in a socialist economy led by Ron, who had been out of work since his defeat in the polls.

These lectures took place at Victoria Park Primary School in Bedminster. I recall sitting on small colourful chairs, designed for children aged seven to eleven, listening to Ron and following his slides on a screen, with around a dozen trade unionists and Labour Party members. In one session, Ron opposed the continuance of a war economy, which involved the massive expenditure on arms as a form of military Keynesianism, in order to prop up capitalism and imperialism. I agreed but was not swayed by the solution he had put forward.

This was a period in which left wing Labour MPs, like Ron and Tony Benn, were advocating *The Alternative Economic Strategy.* Bob Brain did his best to convince me of its merits. I read and thought about it but came to the conclusion that the British solution it proposed, such as import controls combined with increased state intervention to address working-class concerns, evaded tackling the central problem. I argued with Bob that import controls would only invite retaliation by other countries, and history had shown that radical economic and social measures proposed by the Left had nearly always been ignored or watered down when Labour was in power. I remained convinced that a movement able to oppose capitalism in its entirety was needed if we were to transcend the present system and realise socialism. On politics we agreed to differ but worked together amicably on union matters and were good friends.

In August, not long after I had returned to work from a family holiday at Butlins, in the seaside town of Bognor Regis, job description questionnaires were circulated to chapel members for completion. The questionnaire was designed to assist in reviewing the grading of work carried out by chapel members as part of the job evaluation process, a policy towards which I was still uneasy. Members were informed that once the reviews were finished, individuals would be able to appeal if they felt that their post had been incorrectly graded. We assured members that these appeals would not be heard, nor would the new grades be introduced, until management had agreed to equal representation on an appeals panel. Moreover, if the panel could not reach a consensus, we stipulated that the final decision must rest jointly with the union's district secretary and a company director. At the December chapel meeting, an overwhelming majority of members gave the officers the authority to proceed with the project and I committed myself to helping Bob make it a success.

By then, the company was beginning to realise that the clerical chapel, under our leadership, had settled on a systematic strategy of applying legal rights and local agreements, particularly the disputes procedure, to advance the interests of our members. While not particularly exciting, this strategy would prove to be quite effective, though not a substitute for collective action. As well as pushing the company to engage with the job evaluation initiative, the chapel submitted an extension to the closed shop agreement to cover all clerical staff on union negotiated pay grades. The company offered to ballot all staff, insisting that we had to achieve a 75 per cent majority in each individual department. This we said was unacceptable and, applying the disputes procedure, we referred our claim to our new district secretary, Joe Hall, Fred Taylor having retired a couple of months earlier.

By late December, the company had dropped its opposition to extending the closed shop to cover both the customer service and production control departments. This development removed our antipathy towards joining the company's works council because it was no longer seen as a rival employee representative organisation for non-managerial staff. However, Bob and I did not consider it as any positive move towards industrial democracy, though it did provide us an opportunity, with the production chapels, to ask questions and acquire some useful information from management.

Chapter 6

A Testing Time (1980–1982)

1980

The DRG FP clerical chapel began the New Year with a post-entry closed shop covering all grades below managerial and supervisory levels. This meant that after years of agitation we had secured a major achievement. However, the signs that this would be another difficult year became immediately apparent. On 2nd January, just as the print unions started negotiations with the British Printing Industries Federation (BPIF) and the Newspaper Society (NS) on the renewal of their national agreement, the Iron and Steel Trades Confederation (ISTC) declared a national steel strike, the first since 1926. Under the leadership of the union moderate, Bill Sirs, ISTC members walked out in protest against a derisory pay offer of two per cent from the British Steel Organisation, markedly below the current inflation rate of eighteen per cent. The stoppage was to last thirteen weeks.

On my birthday, Sunday 9th March, along with Bob Brain and a few clerical chapel members, I accompanied other Bristol print workers on a coach to London to join a protest rally against the Conservative government's economic and social policies, called by the TUC. For many of the 100,000 present it was a day to show support for the striking steel workers, with a vocal section calling for a General Strike. Two women demonstrators who worked for the British Steel Corporation at Stocksbridge, Sheffield expressed shock at the violence of the police on their picket line and there was anger at the police containment policy as marchers wound their way from Hyde Park to Trafalgar Square.[77]

In Bristol on 2nd April, serious disturbances took place in St Pauls (the local paper described it as a riot) after a drug bust on the Black and White café, which was a favourite place for young people to hang out and socialise. The police arrested and charged the owner with allowing cannabis to be smoked on the premises and forcibly seized large quantities of beer and liquor on the grounds that he did not have a current licence to sell alcohol. This was seen as another example of discriminatory harassment and injustice, triggering a pitched battle between the police and the crowd (black and white) which had gathered outside the café.

It so happened that on that day my wife Chris had called the police because a house she was minding for a friend, who was away on holiday, had been broken into. When I came home a couple of constables had just arrived to investigate. We accompanied them to the home of Chris's friend, which was only a couple of streets away, and we all went in. One of the constables, on spotting a replica ceremonial sword displayed on the hallway wall, remarked "I could use that. There's a riot going on in St Pauls. I can't wait to get down there." He knew, of course, that St Pauls was then a predominately black community. I was disturbed to hear an individual police officer, without any pressure from senior ranking officers, actively seeking to engage in conflict. It confirmed my suspicion that there were some overtly racist officers in the force.

* * *

Towards the end of April, after two months of talks between the print unions and the employers' associations, NATSOPA and SOGAT settled for a 20% wage increase and a phased reduction in the length of the working week from 40 hours to 37½ (including paid meal breaks). As in 1977, the NGA pursued their claim with the employers' associations (the British Printing Industries Federation and the Newspaper Society) independently from NATSOPA and SOGAT. It felt that the 20 per cent offer plus a reduction in hours were insufficient to compensate for the changes in working practices demanded by the employers. Initially it was unsuccessful. Undaunted, the NGA then adopted a strategy of pressurising individual firms to sign separate interim deals, which were set to last until final agreements with the employers' associations had been reached. Whenever they met with opposition the NGA took industrial action, disrupting production with overtime bans and chapel meetings in works time. This strategy was designed to bring the employers' associations to heel, and indeed significant numbers within the associations conceded. But not DRG FP, which was among the firms that were determined to hold out, thus creating divisions in the employers' ranks and the spread of various forms of industrial resistance including selective strikes.[78]

DRG FP was one of the few larger companies to be hit with these kinds of action. In the third week of April, after weeks of disruption to the company's production operations, the managing director, David Richards, sent an open letter to both factory and maintenance staff warning that the damage caused by this action, and the settlement already made between the BPIF and NATSOPA/SOGAT, would have a negative impact on the company's ability to compete with foreign competition. He said that the increase in wage costs must be offset by increased productivity, stating that the company required an increase in "output by at least 14% without incurring any more cost increases". [79] In reality this would involve reducing the size of the labour force along with the abandonment of restrictive practices, such as governing output and limiting access to specific jobs to members of one union. The consequences would be a loss of union controls. He sent a copy of the letter to the office staff affirming that we too had to improve our "efficiency and economic performance." I realised balefully that this was no idle threat.

In the meantime, more companies were conceding to the NGA demands. In an attempt to shore up the damage, the BPIF and the NS called for companies to lock out all NGA printers who refused to revert to normal working; DRG FP willingly complied. The NGA responded by setting up picket lines outside the company premises. SOGAT and NATSOPA instructed their members to carry on working as required under the terms of their new mutually agreed contract. I was saddened to see the divisions between the printing unions widen, both in the company and elsewhere.

However, the BPIF and NS had a similar problem; they could not stop the flow of member firms breaking ranks. These divisions on the employers' side proved crucial. Finally, on 11th May they buckled and met the union's demands. For the time being the NGA resumed normal working. The NGA's industrial muscle and membership loyalty had prevailed. They had achieved a victory, yes, but on a very narrow front and one that would prove to have serious repercussions in the longer term.

The DRG executive served notice that they would leave the BPIF and conduct future pay negotiations with the unions independently. They had a specific project to pursue regardless of the BPIF. Bob and I were concerned that the company intended to computerise office jobs in order to reduce staff numbers. In particular, they were considering systems that could automate material control, production planning, stock records, and order estimating in how to determine selling price decisions and some accounting functions more effectively. However, they were not concerned about the impact of these on the workforce. We were not against adopting new technology; we just wanted the company to share the benefits with our members.

At the March clerical chapel meeting we secured our members' support to boycott the operation of computers, visual display units (VDUs) and any associated training pending agreement with the company which protected jobs and offered the prospect of higher rewards, a shorter working week and a safe working environment. We relayed this policy to management and we also requested permission for Bob, Ron Rich, the health and safety representative, and me to attend a one day a week TUC new technology course, for five weeks, early in the New Year. After some hesitation the company agreed on the basis that we would enter into negotiations and commit ourselves to reaching an accord on its introduction.

The VDUs were delivered, but on our insistence remained unpacked. We silently and surreptitiously kept abreast of developments whilst preparing for the time when the mainframe computer system would become fully operational, which our informants told us could take several months.

I had found that by good fortune the key to my desk also unlocked Ken Shipton's office drawer. By coming in very early in the morning I could carefully look through his papers to see if there was anything of interest concerning company plans to advance the introduction of VDUs. I did get caught once, at 6.30 in the morning, sitting behind Shipton's desk. Luckily it was a chapel member, who did not seem at all curious at what I was doing. We both just laughed at the untimely hour we had come to work.

The NGA's crushing victory over the BPIF preceded the passing of the 1980 Employment Bill, which did not receive Royal assent until August. Under this law, rights to take solidarity action by workers in one organisation in support for workers on strike in another organisation (secondary action) were restricted. Moreover, the legal protection from civil action for trade unions taking secondary action was removed, except in a few exceptional circumstances. This draconian change in employment law prompted the print unions to call on their members to take part in a one day national strike on Wednesday May 14th as part of a 'Day of Action' organised by the TUC in protest against government policies.

Bob and I placed flyers on the union notice board inviting support for the march and rally in Bristol. The company removed them after the High Court ruled that the call to union members to join the day of action was unlawful because it urged workers to break their contracts of employment. To overcome this, we distributed a circular to our members with a detachable form to sign and return to Bob or me if they intended to go, so that we could inform management that they would be absent and did not expect to be paid for that day. As I recall, Bob and I were the only ones from our chapel who struck work for the day and attended the rally.

Embroiled in constant conflict at work I managed to occasionally escape into the absorbing, detached world of chess, which removed me from everyday pressures. During the May spring bank holiday, I was back in Stroud playing in the annual chess tournament and a couple of weekends later I competed in the Bristol open chess congress. I did not perform well in either; nevertheless, I still found satisfaction in winning the odd game.

Back in the real world at DRG FP, David Richards, the managing director, sent a notice, in June, to the office staff stating that the company was 'downsizing' through natural wastage, meaning that when staff left the company they would not be replaced. Bob Brain and I reminded the company that the chapel's policy was not to provide cover for work resulting from an unfilled vacancy. We followed this up with a formal claim to reduce our working hours from a 37½ hour week to a 35 hour one with no reduction in wages. We felt that if the company believed that there was less work to be done then the trouble-free answer would be to cut working hours. Moreover, this would have brought us in line with the machine and finishing chapel members who, as a result of changes to the national agreement, would be working a 35-hour week by July 1982.

In July the company ran a series of assemblies with all of its employees outlining the tough trading conditions it faced both at home and abroad. Against this background it reiterated that "significant improvements in productivity" were necessary. This was the same message it had delivered to all company staff a few months earlier, after NATSOPA and SOGAT had reached their pay settlement with the BPIF. Again, the clerical chapel refused to be cowed. At the 4th September chapel meeting members agreed to continue boycotting the installation of VDUs until a new technology agreement had been signed, and welcomed the news that Bob and I had joined with our counterparts at DRG Cartons and DRG Packaging Bags in our efforts to attain a reduction in working hours for all the Bristol clerical workers employed by the DRG group.

At the same meeting I obtained backing for my motion to call on NATSOPA to support the building of community councils in every major city, to bring together sections of local groups, such as trade unions, tenants' associations, anti-racist organisations and campaigns against police violence. The initiative to form these councils, though other similar ones were around, came from the WRP, who placed Vanessa Redgrave in charge of the project. I had no idea how this sudden shift in WRP policy from one of advocating the taking of power to engaging in a reformist position of working with other groups combating economic and social policies had come about. Opposition came from some Trotskyist organisations, such as the Workers Socialist League who predicted that WRP's Community Councils "would be nothing more than talking shops".[80] However, facing the Tory onslaught on jobs and the decline in workers' standard of living, I firmly believed something had to be done. We needed a broader base for effective resistance, and I thought that the building of community councils could make a positive contribution towards that end.

The impact of the government's policy induced slump—the rise in the operation of market forces, reduction in direct taxes, the increase in indirect taxes and cuts in public spending—was palpable. Unemployment had risen steeply, reaching two million by August 1980, and inflation was running at about eighteen per cent. Manufacturing industry, already in decline, was hit particularly hard during 1980 with the closure of three steel works, Consett, Corby and Shotton, resulting in the loss of 20,000 jobs.

The printing and packaging industry was not immune from this contraction of production, which I knew only too well through my own partially successful attempts to keep the lacquer laminating machines fully occupied. Hence, it was not a total surprise to me to receive, along with the rest of the workforce, notification from David Richards that managers had identified a number of jobs in both the factory and staff areas that were no longer required. Consequently, he declared that approximately 90 people would be made redundant by the end of October.[81] A testing time lay ahead.

The company planned to reduce office staff numbers by 12 out of around 120 and put out a call for volunteers to take early retirement. Bob and I made it clear that the clerical chapel would not accept any form of enforced redundancy and that unless a voluntary solution was found the company could not expect any cooperation from us.

A week later, with the company's permission, 80 union members gathered together in the works canteen for a clerical chapel meeting. Bob gave a brief summary of the talks that had taken place and the terms of the redundancy payment. Twelve white-collar jobs were tabled for redundancy, though the clerical chapel was only expected to submit one, and that one, the company specified, had to come from the wages office. This seemed rather odd to us because the company also indicated that it intended to recruit an additional person in the accounts office but did not offer the possibility of redeployment.

Chapel members were bemused too, and unanimously adopted a motion opposing redundancies and approved a proposal banning overtime in the wages office by 77 votes to 3. This was significant because the wages office staff distributed pay packets (wages were mainly paid in cash in the early 1980s) on overtime to night shift workers.

The following week, further talks were held with management but ended without agreement. The company then served a redundancy notice on the former chair and founder member of the clerical chapel, Roger Vaughan, who worked in the wages office. The other eleven redundancies were deemed to come from middle management and non-unionists. This had a devastating impact on Roger who certainly did not want to leave. Immediately, Bob Brain put out a call for members to attend an emergency chapel meeting at nine o'clock on the morning of 24th October. As we gathered in the room to hear the FoC's address I sensed a dark cloud of fear hanging over my union colleagues.

At the start of proceedings, two chapel members from the buying office proposed that standing orders be suspended, and that all votes must be by a secret ballot; they won the former and lost the latter. Bob then explained that all avenues, including redeployment, had been explored but the company would not budge. We viewed DRG FP's decision as irrational. It looked to us as if management were conducting a personal vendetta against Roger for being an outspoken union member, but the chapel officers needed some ammunition with which to fight the case. Bob then read out the chapel committee's motion for members to consider and vote:

> In view of the failure to reach [a] negotiated settlement the Chapel will take strike action to press for the withdrawal of redundancy to take effect immediately.

This aroused emotions of alarm and anger; after a brief but bitter debate, the motion was put to the vote and lost, 29 for, 36 against and four abstentions.[82]

We were not prepared for this negative result, which was exceedingly difficult to accept. We called an adjournment for a quarter of an hour so that Bob and I could find the least damaging way of implementing what we found was a humiliating and destructive decision. We put together another motion and placed it before the meeting:

> The Chapel reluctantly accepts the fact there is one redundancy and will be seeking the implementation of the 1968 Agreement i.e., last in, first out. We will endeavour to ensure that any Chapel member who is made redundant should be given the opportunity for reinstatement as each future vacancy occurs.[83]

All but one voted to support this proposal as a way forward. Bob and I then asked the members to vote on maintaining the overtime ban in the wages office, which was passed without dissent. These motions of course were token gestures that we knew would not hold. Sadly, Roger, aged 57, was forced to leave and take the lump sum redundancy compensation payment, which was a little more than the statutory amount, and his early retirement pension.

The defeat extended more broadly, and the clerical chapel now found itself seriously vulnerable. Management forced through changes to the organisation of work. The customer service (sales) department was restructured into business groups and the number of sales account executives reduced from 20 to 18. Order clerks were brought together to operate in one order processing section and their contingent was reduced from eight to seven. Estimators too were reorganised into one department and their body cut from ten to nine.

The company took advantage of the weakened authority of the clerical chapel by dismissing its outstanding claim for shorter working hours, though members requested that the chapel officers continue to press for this through the disputes procedure. Keen to get the introduction of the mainframe computer and VDUs up and running, the management did agree to honour their earlier commitment for Bob, Ron Rich, and me to attend a five-week day release course on new technology starting in January.

1981

By the start of the New Year, the Labour Party, now headed by the left leaning Michael Foot, had a 24-point poll lead over the Conservatives[84], giving opposition MPs and trade unions hope of forcing the government to change direction. A spirit of optimism was palpable among fellow shop stewards when I attended the TUC new technology course during January and February. Nevertheless, one particular aspect of Margaret Thatcher's government policy, the right to buy one's council house at a heavily discounted price, was proving very popular, not just with people in general but in my own personal life, for Chris was one among those who wanted to take up the opportunity.

Of course, I was opposed because this would undermine an important source of social housing. I thus faced a moral dilemma. I identified with Chris's right to pursue her wish but felt I would be betraying my principles if I agreed. Chris spent more time at home than me and had shown great tolerance over the years while I was devoting so much of my energy to trade union and political work. After months of consideration, despite my feelings of immense unease, we decided to apply, beginning the long process of determining the discounted price, by arranging a mortgage and addressing all the other legal requirements. It might seem rather foolish, perhaps, to take on a mortgage at a time when job insecurity was increasing, though I could not foresee then that unemployment would grow to levels last seen in the 1930s.

An early and sinister sign appeared in the middle of January, when the British Steel Corporation balloted its employees on its 'survival plan' with the 'choice' of accepting or forcing the corporation into liquidation. They voted in favour, and although the ISTC's ballot of its members voted to reject the plan, the union leadership ruled out industrial action. The subsequent streamlining of British Steel was to lead to 22,000 job losses.

The Thatcher government's policies were geared to the restructuring of Britain's industries in order to make them more competitive and they resonated with the directors of the DRG group. After the BPIF's humiliating retreat in the 1980 annual wage negotiations, DRG announced that future collective bargaining on pay would take place directly between the Group and the print unions. Further, the Group's policy objective now was to move away from national agreements and make local agreements with each individual plant. This decentralisation strategy meant that subsidiary companies within the Group would have more power to make their own decisions in the way they managed their businesses and controlled their costs. One consequence was that only the union stood in the way of local management at DRG FP imposing their will and demanding that we fully cooperate in the introduction of computer technology.

After completing our union course, and evaluating the probable consequences of computerisation, Bob and I drew up a list of demands in the form of a draft new technology agreement. We presented it to management and sent a copy to Joe Hall, the NATSOPA Bristol district secretary, for ratification by the branch committee. The essential requirements in the draft document included no redundancies, no wage cuts, reduction in working hours, exclusive operational rights to NATSOPA members and certain health and safety guarantees, such as free eye tests and the use of swivel chairs.

I realised that to shore up the bargaining position of the clerical chapel in reaching a meaningful accord over the introduction of computer technology, we needed to build alliances with the factory chapels. At its March meeting the clerical chapel supported the proposal, put forward by Brian Brown and me, to

> seek agreement with every production chapel within DRG FP for the adoption of a common policy with regard to the introduction and use of 'new technology' equipment.[85]

In the interim we had to maintain our holding position in order to prevent management from circumventing our boycott on the installation of VDUs. This appeared to be an imminent threat.

The day after our chapel meeting, Hugh Neate, the accounts manager, warned Bob and I that he was going to install a VDU into the accounts office and that by the end of the year there would be eight in operation whether we agreed or not. He was venting his frustration at having been unable to carry out his plans because of the stalemate in the negotiations between the personnel department and the clerical chapel.[86] We took him seriously and sent out a notice to our members reminding them that the chapel policy was to have nothing to do with new technology until an agreement with the company had been concluded.[87]

After a long period of shadow boxing, suddenly a series of exacting developments occurred in swift succession. I had some time out to attend a NATSOPA special governing council as a delegate in the third week of April, just as the annual pay negotiations between DRG and the print unions were being conducted. By early May a pay deal had been reached. While the clerical chapel was party to this, the interpretation on how the pay rates and conditions applied to clerical workers had to be resolved locally through talks between Malcolm Carr, for the company, and Bob and me, for the clerical chapel. The national union officer responsible for leading the pay talks with DRG, John Selby, endorsed our position that we would not "in any way" include other matters, such as the introduction of new technology or other productivity arrangements, as a condition of settlement.[88]

As we feared, during these talks the company tried to bludgeon Bob and I to concede to the deployment of computers and the associated technology as a conditional part of the pay package. It took nine meetings and fifteen hours of discussions over several days to reach an acceptable offer that did not assent to the implementation of new computer systems without the guarantees we had stipulated in our draft agreement. We did consent to "cooperate fully with the company in reaching [a negotiated] agreement on the implementation of revised administrative systems".[89] 'Reaching' of course was the key word, being open to interpretation.

We had no sooner secured this pay settlement when Bob, unexpectedly, told me he was going to stand down as FoC. I was taken completely by surprise. I had no idea he had been contemplating resignation. He had seen the chapel through a tense and difficult period with a level-headed composure. With the June Annual General Meeting (AGM) of the chapel just days away, it was disappointing news. After he had given his FoC's report at the AGM he announced that he would not accept nomination to run as FoC for another year. So, for the third time in seven years I was elected to lead the chapel at a testing time. Fortunately, Bob was persuaded to take on the deputy FoC position. I think his decision must have been because he wanted more time to pursue his political interests and address personal matters.

My election coincided with the arrival of a computer software consultant, Martin Knight of Fraser Williams' Logistics, to discuss DRG

FP's requirements for a Work-in-Progress (WIP) system. I managed to get hold of a copy of the minutes that outlined the headway he had made in designing the system. In Knight's report he expressed concern that he could not consult with NATSOPA clerical chapel members because of our boycott. The minutes inferred that he did not anticipate any similar problem with the NATSOPA machine chapel. He planned to locate a VDU in the WIP store, which factory workers would operate.[90]

This sounded warning bells and I immediately wrote to Joe Hall expressing my concern that the machine chapel had, apparently, not been consulted. I said that I would bring this matter to the attention of the machine chapel's FoC, Malcolm Jenkins, who had succeeded Joe when he left the company to run the Bristol and District branch of NATSOPA at the end of 1979. I also reminded Joe that we were still awaiting responses from the company on outstanding claims they had promised to address in February.

Preparations for the installation required the linking of VDUs through cables to the mainframe computer situated in a large room in the accounts office. Within a week of my letter of concern to Joe Hall, maintenance workers started to lay these cables in the offices. On 23rd June I wrote to the personnel manager, Malcolm Carr, objecting to what I considered was a "hostile action against the clerical chapel" and demanded that this work be halted at once "so that negotiations on an agreement could proceed in a progressive manner".[91] The following day I notified the FoC of the machine chapel, Malcolm Jenkins, of this development and asked for his assistance by instructing his members not to move VDUs, computer terminals or associated equipment into clerical areas.[92]

Over the weekend of 27th and 28th June, when I was happily competing in a chess tournament in Bristol, work on laying cables in the offices had continued. This was an act of overt defiance and I warned Carr that if this action did not cease it would jeopardise talks on negotiating an agreement. A critical stage had been reached. Increasingly it seemed that the company intended to force us into submission. I had to act quickly and sought help from the national union. A meeting was arranged with John Selby, the NATSOPA full-time organiser. Learning that he was already coming to Bristol on 7th July for a meeting with the head of the DRG personnel department at its headquarters in Redcliffe Street, Bob and I, along with other NATSOPA officers from DRG FP, arranged to see him afterwards at the union branch office.

Upon hearing about Selby's forthcoming visit to Bristol, DRG FP's management quickly produced a draft version of so-called "changes in administrative systems"; an emollient phrase to cover what it really meant, the introduction of new technology. The company had clearly cobbled it together in a hurry; it did not meet any of our demands and, after brief consideration, the chapel committee rejected it out of hand.

In the interim, I was able to get hold of a copy of the progress report on the computerisation of the Work-in-Progress (WIP) system. This confirmed that two VDUs and one printer were to be located in the WIP store and that the selection of staff, their training and the programming was due to start in August. The machine chapel seemed oblivious of this and worryingly showed little outward concern.

In a strategic move to garner support I distributed an open letter to non-union staff inviting them to join the NATSOPA clerical chapel and alerting them to the sweeping changes likely to occur as a result of computerisation. I stated that while the clerical chapel recognised the need for change, we were "also conscious of the very real threat to jobs which will emerge in the coming months/years." I added that in the clerical chapel officers' negotiations on the introduction of new technology, our aim was to ensure that we were fully consulted before any new equipment was deployed so that we could secure "guarantees against job losses' and any other adverse developments in order to "safeguard the future of NATSOPA employees". I finished with a call for non-unionists to give "serious thought to the future" and become member of the clerical chapel.[93] No one took up the offer.

The outcome of the discussions with John Selby led to the machine and clerical chapels combining as a bargaining unit to negotiate the introduction of digital technology using the draft agreement that Bob and I had already submitted. This was an important strengthening of forces on the union side. Nevertheless, I foresaw some potential problems. By entering into this partnership, I felt that we had lost an element of control. I did not think the machine chapel was cognisant of the implications of the technological changes the company was planning to usher in. Also, I was unsure whether John Selby fully understood either. Nonetheless, as an act of good faith Bob and I agreed that VDUs, and computer associated equipment could be delivered, provided they were not used and remained under wraps.

This was how the state of affairs stood in the company's push to automate clerical and administrative work when I left work to start a week's holiday on 17th July.

* * *

My summer break with Chris and the girls came in the midst of this period of intense union activity. The previous year I had bought a second hand four berth framed tent from Brian Brown, which we had used on weekend trips to Burnham-on-Sea and Brean in Somerset. This year we had booked ahead to camp on a site in Croyde Bay, North Devon. By coincidence, when we arrived, we found that Brian was also staying on the same site with his wife, Joan, and fourteen-year-old daughter, Julie. Despite being opposed to many of one another's views, thrown together by chance we found that we could both adapt and transcend our differences. During the week, a jellyfish stung Julie, on the leg while she was swimming in the sea and he asked me for help, because she could not walk unaided. With an arm around both Brian and I, we transported her to my car and took her to the local hospital for treatment. I would come to see her again in 1985 as a DRG FP employee and one of our youngest clerical chapel members.

* * *

Within a few days of returning from my vacation, I discovered that Hugh Neate had been testing the new equipment, thereby breaking the agreement I had made with Malcolm Carr that none of the computer hardware kit would be unpacked and used. Incensed, on Friday morning 31st July I called a chapel committee meeting, without requesting time off, to discuss the matter. As a result of our deliberations, I sent a letter to Carr informing him that unless this breach was rectified all negotiations on the proposed introduction of new technology would cease.[94] The machines were switched off on Monday.

We held two further unauthorised meetings, one on Monday morning, the other on Tuesday morning, to work out on what terms we would resume talks with management. Next, we were summoned to the personnel office to explain why, on three occasions, we had walked off our jobs to sit in session. Carr, adopting a headmaster's cold and serious tone, opened up by saying he could not accept company employees absenting themselves from work without permission, thereby breaking their contractual obligations. Our chairman, Brian Brown, put our case by explaining that due to the company violating a pact it had with the clerical chapel, "an emergency existed and had to be treated accordingly." I then asked for the original agreement to be honoured so that negotiations could proceed jointly with the machine chapel. Arrangements were made for Bob and me to have further talks with Hugh Neate. As officers of the machine chapel had endorsed our response, we insisted that this time they should be present. On parting, Carr warned that any future breaches of our employment contracts would result in disciplinary action.[95]

Ensuring that the machine chapel collaborated with us in talks was a step forward because the company had chosen to ignore the fact that the NATSOPA chapels at DRG FP had formed a joint bargaining unit to negotiate an agreement on the installation and use of computer based systems. On Wednesday 5th August, machine chapel officers accompanied Bob Brain and me to talks with Hugh Neate. He set out his case for wanting the computer systems to be turned on for testing and programming. (In response to my complaint, they had been switched off for two days.) We said if he put this in writing and the company removed the threat of disciplinary action against clerical chapel officers then we would consider his request.[96]

Hugh Neate then, grudgingly, provided us with a typed list of reasons as to why he wished to use the computer system, but made no mention of our demand to erase from the record the warnings given to the chapel committee for unauthorised absence from our work stations. We stuck to our explanation that we had met in response to a violation of the company's agreement not to use the new computer equipment. Therefore we refused to consider his request until this injustice was rectified. An incensed Hugh Neate scribbled a note to say he was still awaiting my reply. The company did not tolerate the resulting stalemate for long. After a few days I was notified that it would carry on with computer tests regardless of our protests, though a rider was added saying that it still intended to negotiate a final agreement.

In between these tense exchanges, I was taken somewhat by surprise when the company's laboratory assistants approached me and asked if I would address them about the possibility of joining the clerical chapel. I gathered them together in one of the training rooms I had booked, gave them an overview of the union, made them aware of recent events and said I would love the opportunity to represent them. All six laboratory assistants, five junior and one senior, signed up. A couple of days before taking another week's leave, I wrote to Malcolm Carr and our district branch secretary, Joe Hall, providing them with the names of these new members and requested that the company supply their job descriptions and arrange a meeting to discuss their grading and salary.[97]

During the last week of August, while I was away with my family camping in the Forest of Dean, the company sent an open letter to all clerical and factory staff inviting them to apply for voluntary early retirement/redundancy. In my absence Bob, my deputy, assured our members that the company had not notified NATSOPA officials that there were to be job losses. As the union *Redundancy Agreement* made this a requirement we would not participate in any negotiations.

As soon as I returned, Bob advised me of this unwelcome news and his response. Coming so soon after the last batch of job losses, the continuation of the recession and the growth of unemployment both nationally and locally, it felt as if we were under siege. I wrote to the factory FoCs calling for the formation of an Occupation Committee. In the event of closure, I said

> the committee would appoint groups of workers to inspect the company's books and end the financial secrecy of management. It would organise the occupation of the factory and the maintenance of equipment until such time [as] it [could] be reopened.[98]

I was aware that this radical measure stood little chance of support; however I was trying to get across the message that the post-war social consensus was well and truly finished. We faced an offensive in which the labour movement was in danger of being completely marginalised.

Under the Thatcher government, a major shift in political and economic policy, heavily influenced by neoliberal ideology, was being installed, which ushered in mass unemployment, job flexibility, casual work, greater inequality and poverty. Its aim was to revamp capitalism by mounting a sustained attack on the power trade unions had acquired to defend workers in the previous decade. Workers and their unions faced a stark choice: reject and resist the demands of employers, and risk company closures and job losses, such as those that occurred at British Steel, or accept employers' policies of intensifying work, and capping or cutting wages.

While I was away, Bob had written to the technical manager, Chris Shinner, who had been most put out when he discovered that his laboratory assistants had joined the clerical chapel, informing him that our health and safety officer, Ron Rich, had arranged a safety inspection of the laboratory for the 1st September, the day I was due back.[99] Shinner blocked this from going ahead and sent me a curt letter, endorsed by Malcolm Carr, vehemently insisting that the clerical chapel did not have the right either by written agreement or by implication to represent technical staff and neither was it "the intention of Management to offer such recognition".[100]

After reading this on the morning of my return, I responded immediately advising him that I did not accept his take on this matter, and that I had passed on his note to NATSOPA's district branch secretary. In the meantime, I told him that I would be representing union members in his department.[101] I then promptly reordered a health and safety inspection of the laboratory, which this time Shinner reluctantly felt obliged to accept, causing him some embarrassment. Within a few weeks he realised the futility of his opposition to his laboratory assistants' wishes and conceded representational rights to the NATSOPA clerical chapel.[102]

Occupational health and safety was one area that the company had to take seriously. The Health and Safety at Work Act, 1974, required most employers to carry out a risk assessment so we were able to get the company to finance an independent expert to assess the health and safety requirements in the positioning and use of VDUs. In return, as an act of good faith, I gave the company approval to go ahead with testing and programming the computer systems.[103] Just as I thought we were making progress, the company declared twelve redundancies in the offices, some of which were expected to come from the clerical chapel. Three members volunteered to go. We endorsed their applications on the basis of management's commitment that there would be no compulsory redundancies for at least six months after their departure at the end of November.[104]

This time the factory floor escaped redundancies and the officers of the machine chapel were free to accompany Bob and me in a series of negotiations with Malcolm Carr about the deployment of computer technology. By the fourth week of November these lengthy talks had broken down. This coincided with the period when the testing and programming of the computer systems had been completed. They were now regarded as ready to run.[105]

Ironically, within a couple of days the draft disputes procedure, to which we had been trying to get the company to adhere for several months, was finally agreed. It transpired that the head of DRG personnel, under pressure from the NATSOPA district branch committee, had imposed it on local management. Thus, after the collapse of talks with the company over computerisation, resolution was sought through the disputes procedure. This opened up an alternative means of resolving how computers would be introduced.

Even though this process was very bureaucratic and time consuming, it proved to be an invaluable asset for the clerical chapel. The disputes procedure made any change in working practices inadmissible until all sides could reach a consensus. By freezing the situation, it meant that the status quo prevailed, so that the company was not able to force our members to operate its new computer system after all. Moreover, I was able to channel other outstanding disputes through the various stages of this 'official' route, which helped to allay departmental managers' authority over their staff.[106] The peculiar stasis that ensued proffered the clerical chapel committee a much needed breathing space.

1982

By early January, the clerical chapel had accumulated a backlog of outstanding disputes with the company. Some concerned individual employment grievances; others involved protecting members' interests as a collective body. Due to management prevarication, these were all very slowly making their way through various stages of the disputes procedure, and hence I found myself under increasing pressure in trying to balance my union work with carrying out my scheduling job. The complexity and call on my time as FoC was demanding but I was determined that the union would play a greater role in *establishing* the conditions under which our members worked, rather than constantly fending off management. I aimed to prioritise and pursue the collective interests of the chapel, giving precedence to securing a new technology agreement over personal grievances. In practice, however, this proved to be somewhat problematic.

The trickiest individual case was the discrimination and victimisation against a chapel committee member, Gwen Cheetham. This manifested itself in terms of a personal complaint but had wider significance. Bullying, harassment and discrimination are common sources of intense grievances and in this particular case there was an added trade union factor.

Gwen worked in the typing pool, which had a long history of a repressive culture. In the 1960s and 70s, RWP typists had worked under a severe disciplinary regime that compelled them to adhere to a strict dress code. An anti-trade union atmosphere fostered deference and submission. Consequently, some derided trade unions, while others feared repercussions would follow if they joined a union.[107] Since Gwen's election as a chapel officer, she had experienced hostility from her supervisor, who opposed the union. It became increasingly difficult for her to have any time off to deal with emergencies at home with her family.

When one such urgent situation arose, her supervisor refused to grant her request for a day's leave. Gwen had spent the night to comfort and support her sister who was ill in hospital. Early the following morning she rang her supervisor saying she was going home to sleep but was denied permission. Gwen responded in desperation by taking a day's holiday. I spent a great deal of time with her discussing how to resolve this matter, and other abrasive incidents she had been subjected to. Gwen was adamant: "You've got to do something about it Mike. I will not put up with her [the supervisor] any longer. I'm not prepared to work in the typing pool office in any circumstance." Accompanied by Bob, I spoke to the personnel manager, Malcolm Carr, advocating Gwen's demand that she should be redeployed to another department. This was rejected. Instead Carr wanted to discipline Gwen for taking time off without the company's approval. Bob pointed out that disciplinary measures would require her to be represented by Joe Hall, the NATSOPA Bristol and district branch secretary because she was an elected official of the chapel.[108]

Several meetings with, and letters to, Malcolm Carr, protesting about the discriminatory actions of Gwen's supervisor yielded nothing. We were making no headway, so I compiled a list of the clerical chapel's claims and complaints and I sent them to Joe Hall to take up with the DRG personnel department at their head office in Redcliffe Street. Gwen's grievance, along with other demands, thus moved to a new formal stage of the disputes procedure to be dealt with by senior personnel managers and a full-time union official. In reaching this stage the chapel commended Bob and I for the way we had conducted its "affairs in extremely difficult and tense times."[109] This support was gratifying. It acknowledged that we were endeavouring as best we could to have an effect in what was an exceedingly frustrating and wearing period. I felt that the company's actions were aimed specifically at preventing the chapel from gaining any meaningful influence. I believed that Gwen's case was an example of the company adopting intimidatory tactics against a chapel representative. It echoed the threatening behaviour of my manager, Ken Shipton, when I had taken on the mantle of FoC for the second time in 1975.

On 28th January, talks with the personnel department at DRG's head office eventually yielded a commitment to hasten the resolution of outstanding matters. This included consent to the temporary transfer of Gwen to another department until a company investigation into our assertions had been carried out. Geoff Haigh, the Group personnel manager, came up with a circumlocutory assurance that delays were not part of DRG FP's policy and his hopes for improvement. He added that "all manager's authority [was] circumscribed to some extent" and now that we had the formal disputes procedure, the company would "try to do better."[110] Another meeting was arranged to review what progress had been made.

Despite Haigh's conciliatory emollience, back at DRG FP the atmosphere was sour. When a young woman moved out of the post room to fill a vacancy in the accounts office, Malcolm Carr rejected our demand to recruit a replacement to restore the post room staffing levels back to three. He also refused to acknowledge that the status quo clause in the disputes procedure, accepted by management, required that this should be done. I had little option but to write directly to Haigh expressing my annoyance that the management at DRG FP was still prevaricating. An exchange of letters followed as well as more meetings.[111] On 18th February, at the Group's head office, Haigh again pledged that the company would honour the status quo clause, only for the DRG FP to renege on this promise the following day. My response was swift.

On Wednesday 24th February, I instructed clerical union members to boycott post room work handled by non-union staff. Tensions rose as management and non-unionists tried to pressurise union members into disregarding my directive. I spent a significant amount of my time picketing the dispute and safeguarding my members from intimidation by both management and some non-unionists. Despite the threats, chapel members maintained the ban.

On Friday the company backed down and offered to recruit a commercial trainee. I accepted this compromise resolution on the basis that for a significant part of the working week this trainee would provide assistance in the post room. On these grounds the dispute was settled, though my manager, Ken Shipton, gave me a verbal warning for failing to carry out my normal duties during the dispute because I had spent an excessive amount of time policing the post room boycott. I ignored it. The lesson I took from this battle of wills was that the chapel had to be prepared to take direct action in order to exert enough influence to get the company to yield.

The post room staffing question was important because it was about defending the interests of union members from additional performance pressures and job losses, as well as providing work for a school leaver at a time of high youth unemployment. The benefit of being able to maintain the status quo through the disputes procedure was proving to be a crucial aid. This is why Bob and I were so resolute in preserving it. In March, after talks had collapsed over the introduction of computer aided systems, the status quo clause provided the chapel with an important source of leverage once again. It enabled the chapel to 'legitimately' continue its ban on the use of new computer equipment. This proved to have significant repercussions. In exasperation the company decided to circumvent the disputes procedure and go over the heads of the chapel officers. Angered by my insistence to stick to the guarantees stipulated in our draft agreement, the company tried to turn the tables by appealing directly to the chapel membership.

In the third week of March, in an open letter, the managing director, David Richards, informed clerical chapel members that the union negotiated annual wage increase, due to be paid in April, would be withheld. He stated that "it would be unreasonable to expect the Company to commence a further review of salaries for 1982 until an agreement on changed administrative systems [new technology] has been concluded." He urged the chapel "to reconsider their views" as the company could ill-afford "to have expensive [computer] equipment … remaining unused."[112]

A few days after the managing director's manoeuvre, 53 members, out of a possible 73, assembled for a chapel meeting. I revealed to them that David Richards failed to include in his 'open letter' that the company had insisted on including a six month exit clause on the job security safeguard we had specified in our version of a new technology agreement. After a short discussion the chapel unanimously reaffirmed support for the draft new technology agreement we had presented to the company in early 1981 and voted to support Bob and me in our continuing efforts to obtain the guarantees we had laid down.[113] I updated Joe Hall and reminded him that the machine chapel's pay award had not been withheld. He, in turn, informed the national officer, John Selby, of these developments. I also added that until the threats contained in David Richards' letter were removed, we would not return to the negotiating table.

Nevertheless, Selby went ahead and organised a meeting with the company for 23rd April. He did, however, promise to raise our demand prior to the commencement of talks. Bob and I, representing the clerical chapel, and the machine chapel's FoC and deputy, accompanied Selby, who led our delegation. The talks ended in deadlock and a failure to agree was registered. In an exchange of letters between Selby and Richards, outlining the areas of disagreement, Selby warned that as the company was refusing to implement the clerical wage increases that had been due to be paid on 24th April, he would refer this "hostile act" to the NATSOPA Executive Council.[114] On 12th May, Richards replied that the company was prepared to move to the final stage of the disputes procedure, involving arbitration between DRG's chief executive, Moger Woolley, a former DRG FP managing director, and the NATSOPA general secretary Owen O'Brien.[115] But in the meantime the company still refused to implement our pay increases.

The negotiating process had become confused. Selby's proposal was at odds with my commitment to the clerical chapel that we would not return to the negotiating table until the company agreed to implement the 1982 wages award. Moreover, the dispute came at a particularly inconvenient time because the National Executive and full-time officials of NATSOPA had begun vying for positions in what was to become a new amalgamated print union under the name of SOGAT 82.

Richards sought to take advantage of NATSOPA's internal distractions by attempting to drive a wedge between union members and their elected officers. On Friday 14th May, in another open letter to clerical chapel staff, he accused chapel officers and branch officials of failing to keep a promise we had given in the 1981 pay settlement, that the company "would be able to work the new equipment".[116] This was untrue. Our only commitment had been to cooperate in *reaching* a negotiated agreement.

We were approaching a critical moment at work and I was right in the middle of it. At home over the weekend, I mulled over what to do while trying to perfect my dart throwing technique. Not only did darts help me to reduce my stress levels and enhance my ability to think more clearly by focusing on the board, I realised that playing with confidence was key. Somehow, I had to apply this in dealing with the approaching crisis and not be distracted. The responsibility was daunting.

On 18th May I called an emergency chapel meeting. Without the company's permission 65 chapel members stopped work to attend. The high turn out indicated the strength of resentment provoked by the managing director's coercive and bullying approach. His attitude did much to remove any vestige of his superior status that some clerical chapel members may have held. I told my members frankly that the company was trying to blackmail us into accepting the introduction of computer assisted systems on detrimental terms by withholding our annual wage award. In the process it was also trying to break the clerical and machine chapel bargaining unit, for the NATSOPA factory workers had not been subjected to the same hostile treatment.

Knowing the reticence of chapel members to support an all-out stoppage of work, I proposed that the chapel agree to take selective strike action—bringing out a tactical group of workers in a key area—who I would select in consultation with the chapel committee, at an 'appropriate' time. The rest of the chapel, if necessary, would then finance these members. This was put to the vote and carried, 60 in favour, 4 against and 1 abstention, a ringing endorsement.[117]

The following day members who had attended the emergency union meeting were cautioned for being absent without official permission. Twenty four hours later, the personnel manager, Malcolm Carr, accompanied by his assistant, Sue Watson, and my manager Ken Shipton, reminded me that because I had been reprimanded for neglecting my normal duties during the recent post room dispute, on this occasion I was to be given a written warning for being absent a second time without notice. I refused to recognise its legitimacy because there was no Bristol branch officer present. As an elected SOGAT FoC,

I had a right to call on one to represent me. I then formally appealed on behalf of my chapel members against the verbal admonishments that management had meted out to them the previous day.

My job now was to contact the factory chapels for backing. The FoCs of NATSOPA, SOGAT and the NGA agreed to cooperate. My plan was to pull out on strike ten members of the clerical chapel working in production control, including myself. This would have an immediate impact, as factory production would quickly grind to a halt if union members on the shop floor refused to take instructions and relevant documentation from office managers and non-unionists.

On 19th May I wrote to Malcolm Carr requesting yet again that the company "honour the annual wage settlement and implement payment immediately or face the consequences of industrial action." David Richards reacted by writing yet another open letter, this time to the whole of the workforce. He outlined the "tough trading conditions" faced by the company and declared that the best way to

> ensure the future of the business is by offering materials to our customers at competitive prices, while giving them good service and good quality. Actions or disruption which adversely affect any of these…
>
> [would] threaten the company and the livelihoods of its employees. …
>
> I ask you to consider this very carefully, so that we can work to secure the future together.[118]

Two clerical chapel members decided to resign from the union as a result of this letter.

After a weekend of nervous deliberations, culminating in a chapel committee meeting at Bob Brain's house, we decided to launch our selective strike plan on the following morning, Monday 24th May. When the time came to start work, I pulled out ten members, including myself, from the production control office and marched them down through the factory to the canteen rest room. By the time we had reached our destination, shut the door and settled in some comfy chairs, the word of our action had got around. I left my deputy, Bob Brain, to explain to management what was happening.

DRG FP clerical chapel strike (participants) March 1982. Left to right back row: Ron Rich, Colin Gould, Graham White. Left to right front row: Jackie Turnham, Leslie Gibbens, Mike Richardson (FoC), Graham Reynolds, June Barnard, Brian Brown.

Before long our first visitor arrived, Peter Hopkins, a member of the NATSOPA machine chapel who worked as an assistant on the lacquer laminating machines. I knew him well and had had many political debates with him. He was a member of his local Liberal Party so unsurprisingly we had many political differences. Nevertheless, as a loyal and outspoken trade unionist, he had come to inform me that our stoppage was already having an impact and expected that the majority of lacquer coating and lacquer laminating machines would have run out of work by the end of the day.

A new member of the production control office, Jackie Turnham, had only started at the company at the end of April, joining the union soon afterwards. And now she was out on strike. She told me that she had passed her 'A' levels the previous year, including one in sociology as I recall. Regardless of her youth I was impressed by the intelligence she displayed throughout the extraordinary events that followed, and even more remarkably by her maturity in making decisions. She would go on to become a friend and a loyal supporter of the union.

When Bob Brain popped his head in to make sure we were okay, he had nothing to report at his end except to say how quiet it was in the production control office, which was normally abuzz with noise and vibrancy. This was not a sit-in; it was a protest strike. Sit-ins involve taking possession of a factory or workplace. This we did not do. By striking we breached our terms of employment as a protest against the company failing to honour a pay settlement agreement negotiated by our union. There was no picket line. Support from the shop floor unions had been secured before we took action.

We ate our lunch in the works canteen (cooked and served by SOGAT members) and up to the time we left for home at 5pm we had heard nothing from the management. I found this somewhat unsettling, trying to guess their response. When we arrived the next morning, apart from the sound of workers' chatter the majority of the factory was silent. We resumed our place in the rest room, which was turning into a kind of social hub.

My striking colleagues brought in playing cards and the word game, scrabble, to while away the hours. Bob Palmer, a clerical chapel committee member, dropped in to take some photographs. Then in quick succession came George Bly, the deputy FoC of the NATSOPA machine chapel, the NGA FoC, John Price, and my friend Jim Cox, the NGA chapel secretary. Their visits were uplifting as were the donations for our dispute fund. We received £50 from the machine chapel and £20 from the DRG Cartons and Printing NATSOPA machine chapel, where my old work colleague from the 1960s, Andy Pickford, happened to be the deputy FoC. Seeing him again and finding ourselves working for the same organisation, belonging to the same union and fighting the same battles, strengthened my resolve.

Behind the scenes there was a lot of activity. We were picking up news of crisis talks. Moger Woolley, DRG's Chief Executive, was called back from a meeting in York for talks with the union hierarchy, including the NATSOPA general secretary, Owen O'Brien. This brought immediate results. During Wednesday 26th May, I received a personal message from O'Brien, via our staunch ally, Joe Hall, that the company had now agreed to implement the terms of the annual wage settlement backdated to the 24th April. As the cause of the dispute had been settled, O'Brien ordered that "all members of the Chapel to return to

DRG FP clerical chapel strike, March 1982, scrabble game.

normal working forthwith." He expressed grave concern about DRG FP's future, which he had been informed was "in a very delicate balance" and, as a consequence, the company had decided "not to proceed with the implementation of new technology at this stage."[119] This was an exceedingly significant announcement.

Owen O'Brien was not happy that we had struck work before he had a chance to have talks with the company. Ominously, he was aware that restrictive legislation was impending. As it turned out our timing of industrial action proved to be impeccable. If the 1982 Employment Bill had already become law, most probably, before taking up our case, he would have ordered us back to work. A key aspect of the new law was to remove trade unions' immunity from certain actions 'in tort'. This meant that strikes preventing companies from lawfully operating their businesses could be construed as a civil wrong; hence employers could obtain injunctions against unions and sue them for damages. This anti-union legislation received Royal assent at the end of October.

We were thus fortunate in our timing, but the decisive element was the support we received from the shop floor. I had realised that only by stopping production could we succeed. The selective strike had proved effective. By bringing out workers in the clerical chapel involved in organising the production process, we had opened the way.

There was no cheering, singing or dancing when the news came through that the company had conceded. We were happy of course but we had to immediately return to our desks in the production control office and resume normal working and I did not want us to revel in victory. I felt it important to show restraint. I wanted non-unionists to see the validity of our case. Nonetheless, an uneasy atmosphere pervaded the production control office. When we returned, I sensed senior staff felt that top management had capitulated and in doing so had undermined their position of authority.

Whether an awareness of this resentment influenced David Richards' decision to uphold the verbal warnings given to chapel members, for attending an unauthorised meeting during working hours on 18th May, is difficult to tell. I wrote to him saying that I would appeal against his 'final' decision through the disputes procedure. I also sought Joe Hall's opinion. However, Joe was in the process of becoming an area officer in our new amalgamated union, SOGAT 82, so he passed my letter on to our new SOGAT 82 branch secretary, Joe Selway. He considered that we should leave an appeal in abeyance while the position of the company's future was unclear.

SOGAT's and NATSOPA's futures lay in their unification as SOGAT 82. As a delegate to the NATSOPA governing council I went to its last meeting in mid June at the Winter Gardens in Margate. On Wednesday 16th June a commemoration dinner marked the occasion. I returned from this final gathering of the NATSOPA delegates in a celebratory mood. At last unity between NATSOPA and SOGAT had been effected through SOGAT 82. Back at work I learned that the company had made arrangements for the FoCs of the major unions in DRG FP to attend a full day's symposium at the DRG staff college at Abbots Leigh, on 5th July. Although not specified, I felt that this was going to be a crisis meeting about the steps the company proposed to take to revive its business and halt the decline in profits. Three familiar prophets of doom, the Chief Executive of the DRG group, Moger Woolley, David Richards, and Arthur Grinham, the Group's divisional accountant, were scheduled, to address the meeting.

It seemed so strange to me, after returning from a special ceremonial occasion, that I, along with other FoCs, was mingling with a group of the company's top managers, consuming tea and biscuits before being given 'reality facts' which we were simply expected to accept. Formal presentations were interspersed with informal talks in the coffee and lunch breaks. The company pressed home its key points, a reduction in the numbers employed, the removal of so called 'restrictive' practices and the acceptance of changes in technology. Moger Woolley and his colleagues proposed meeting again, if they received a favourable response from the union general secretaries involved to help resolve the financial problems the company faced. They had already organised to see them on 9th July when, with their agreement, a follow up meeting at Abbotts Leigh training college was arranged for the 12th August. Management was clearly taking a new tack.

Then, during July, a couple of discrimination cases arose. The first occurred a couple of weeks before I was due to take my summer vacation. After a tip-off from one of our members, Bob and I warned the company that it would be a breach of the Equal Opportunities Act if we found it to be true that female applicants for a vacant scheduling post would not be considered.[120] Unfortunately, we did not have any hard evidence and a man filled the position through an internal transfer while I was on holiday in the last week of July. It was becoming noticeable that management initiatives tended to coincide with my time off work!

*   *   *

Chris was really looking forward to our summer vacation in 1982. Since February she had been working evenings as a care assistant at a Council run elderly people's home in Highridge, Bristol, a hard and demanding job and one that I knew I could not do. She was still learning how to see to the basic needs of the residents while dealing with her emotional reactions to those struggling with ill health, loneliness and separation from their families. Care workers, like Chris, were expected to manage residents with incontinence and dementia even though they had not received sufficient training. She needed a break more than I did. We took the children, Amanda aged twelve and Jacqui aged eight, to Butlins at Pwllheli, on the coast of North Wales, popular with working-class families with young children.

Though the girls loved it there, we experienced one frightening moment while we were relaxing one day on a beach not far from the holiday camp. Jacqui had been floating close to the shoreline in an inflatable dingy when she dropped her oar over the side. As we watched she started to drift slowly out to sea. Chris and I rushed into the water, but I could not (and still cannot) swim. Chris started to swim towards her. Not making much headway, she realised that Jacqui needed to abandon the dingy. Thinking quickly, she yelled "jump into the water and swim." Chris made her way out to meet her and they returned safely to the shore. Although the whole incident was over in minutes, we were all shaken by what might have happened. I was especially shocked because I tended to feel responsible for taking action, yet had been powerless.

* * *

In my absence from work, my deputy, Bob, had to deal with another case of discrimination. He wrote to the personnel manager complaining that in the course of an interview for a sales executive vacancy, a woman chapel member was asked whether she intended to start a family. He sought an assurance that there [would] be no repetition of this incident and that all management representatives [should be] made fully aware of the provisions of the Sex Discrimination Act 1975.

> [The chapel's] main concern however is that this incident reflects an underlying prejudice within the company with regard to promoting women to senior positions…[121]

These accusations were met with denial and silence and again, in the absence of independent evidence, it was a case of one person's word against another's. Frustrating though this had been, our attention soon turned to the second crisis meeting on the 'state of the business' with top management.

Our muted celebration of victory after our selective strike in May had been prudent. The outcome of the follow-up meeting at Abbots Leigh training college was that the company offered four propositions to secure the viability of the company. The options were grim: (1) a 25% wage cut (2) 200 redundancies (3) 10% wage cut and 50 redundancies (4) 100 redundancies plus a big package of efficiency savings.[122] I along with the rest of the FoCs rejected all these. Yet another session was arranged for 8th September at which David Richards announced the company's definitive survival plan, 132 redundancies and a 'savings' package to include the introduction of new technology.

Henceforth, attacks on workers' jobs and livelihoods at DRG FP became relentless. We were not alone. The local rate of unemployment in Bristol was 11½ per cent. By September, national unemployment had reached over three million and inflation was running at around eight per cent. On the 22nd, the TUC called for a day of action in support of the National Health Service (NHS) workers in their pay dispute. The new SOGAT 82 (hereafter referred to as SOGAT) national executive directed its members to strike on that day. This was a very important recognition that workers were affected by social welfare provision as well as by pay and conditions in the workplace.

A concomitant proposal at our September chapel meeting was approved, instructing me to write to the national executive requesting that exemptions to taking strike action should be given for all those places of work where redundancies had been declared. I sent this appeal to the executive council via the joint general secretaries of SOGAT, Owen O'Brien and Bill Keys. They turned it down. When I took this news to my members a petition was raised forcing me to call an emergency chapel meeting to discuss the matter two days before the strike in support of NHS workers was due.

Janet St. George, who had been elected as chair at the June AGM, presided. I opened the meeting by endorsing the executive council's decision, stressing the importance of the NHS and the need to protect it against the privatisation plans of the Conservative government. I also argued that this was a time to show solidarity, especially as the company were in the throes of making redundancies. Then Janet, departing from the protocol of neutrality expected of the chair, spoke passionately about supporting NHS workers. This unleashed an outburst of opposition to the union's directive that led the former chair of our chapel, Brian Brown, to assert that the new amalgamated union was void of the democratic process.

Regardless of our conflicting political outlooks, I had come to respect Brian, particularly for taking part in our May selective strike, but I could not leave his remarks unchallenged. I reacted somewhat angrily, disputing his claim, pointing out under its rules the SOGAT executive had the right to call a strike and that the whole of the workforce on the shop floor would be out. A vote was demanded which the chair, Janet St. George, on my advice, denied because chapel rules or decisions could not override those of the executive council. This was a chastening experience for me, especially following our successful strike

Janet St. George working on the switchboard.

in May.[123] Upset by Brian's intervention, the next day I reported him to the SOGAT Bristol and the West of England branch committee for actively encouraging chapel members to disobey an executive council ruling.[124]

On the day of action 52.7 per cent of clerical chapel members either struck work, were out sick or on a pre-booked holiday. Disappointingly, five of the production control staff, including Brian Brown, defied the SOGAT edict and turned up for work along with 29 others.[125] I thought their action was selfish. I was deeply disappointed and concerned that it would weaken SOGAT's authority, and mine, in future negotiations with the company. I felt I had to do something to stop this discord because I believed it could well lead to the decline of the chapel as an effective force.

On 24th September I reported all those who failed to comply with the union directive to Joe Selway, the Bristol and West of England branch secretary. This had been a difficult decision, but members had been prewarned of my intentions at the emergency chapel meeting, prior to the day of action. The tensions of conflict when we had gained ascendency had been real enough, but the distress caused by internal division was, of course, far harder. I was upset that around half of my members could not sacrifice one day's pay in support of NHS staff, especially as it was known that all SOGAT members on the factory floor had accepted the ruling to stop work for the day. Inevitably this affair diverted us from the critical problems we faced, especially redundancies.

A few days later Bob and I were informed that thirteen jobs had to go in the areas we represented. Consequently, throughout the coming months our time was to be devoted to consulting with our members over redundancies and the company's associated survival plan. The latter was brought to a head when, in the third week of November, the company insisted that, as part of its reorganisation and cost cutting exercise, the computerised equipment and systems had to be introduced "with immediate effect", and without the guarantees we had demanded.[126] Malcolm Carr relayed this message to both the clerical and machine chapels.

Early the following week the SOGAT clerical, machine and finishing chapel officers met to discuss this development and agreed that we should dismiss the company's demands, and that I was to contact a national union officer in order to restart negotiations on a new technology agreement based on the draft that Bob and I had first drawn up in the early months of 1981.[127]

On 29th November, DRG FP officially declared to the Secretary of State for Employment that it was making over 90 employees redundant. The legal requirement was that the Secretary of State should be notified of collective redundancy, of between 20 and 99 employees, at least 30 days before any dismissals could take effect. But by Christmas the company had still failed to consult or negotiate with us or reply to our counter proposals.

Chapter 7

Struggle and Strife (1983–1987)

1983

On returning from my Christmas holidays, I faced the unenviable task of dealing with redundancies and responding to the company's survival plan. For the foreseeable future the outlook for workers employed at DRG FP looked bleak. Some older clerical chapel members put forward their names to be considered for voluntary early retirement, including our health and safety representative, Ron Rich. A few other younger members had expressed an interest but were waiting to see what financial compensation package they would receive. A couple of others were looking at the prospect of redeployment to a job on the shop floor where the machine and finishing chapels had an excess of volunteers.

With this knowledge the company gave an assurance of no compulsory redundancies in return for cooperation on redeployment and the signing of a pact by all the major unions on a 'survival plan'.[128] If we could deliver sufficient volunteers to go, I sensed that the clerical chapel still had some bargaining power over the introduction of computer aided systems. In fact, even before we finalised our list of volunteers, we struck a new technology agreement almost identical to the draft we had submitted in early 1981. While we had to drop our claim for shorter hours, we did secure exclusive rights for SOGAT members to operate computer assisted equipment. Moreover,

> the introduction of each new piece of equipment or modification of existing equipment [was] to be the subject of a written agreement. Pending an agreement, the status quo [would] apply.[129]

To establish a significant degree of job control in an unfavourable industrial relations climate was, I felt, quite an achievement. Why the company finally decided to settle this long-running dispute at this time was, I believe, strategic.

Also linked to the survival plan was the introduction of a job evaluation scheme, first championed by Bob Brain, in which the union had an equal input in the assessment of clerical grades. The job evaluation panel consisted of two officers of the clerical chapel, the FoC and one other, and two managers directly responsible for clerical staff, though one of them had to be a sitting member of the management committee, a governing body with ultimate responsibility for directing the activity of the company.[130]

In return for these concessions, we accepted the reorganisation of work, administrative systems and the reallocation/transfer of certain employees to alternative positions in the clerical area. I kept my scheduling role but was transferred from planning the work of the lacquer laminating machines to arranging the finishing operations, a less interesting and demanding role. By the end of February, we had accepted the loss of ten people from the chapel; eight volunteered to take redundancy and two were redeployed to jobs on the factory floor. It was extremely regrettable to have lost these members, but I took some solace from the favourable agreements we had made and the fact that as a chapel we still had an effective voice.

My office manager, Ken Shipton, was among those forcibly made redundant. Given our personal history, my response was ambivalent. Ironically, his final words to me were that he should "have joined the NGA". The former technical manager, Chris Shinner, filled his position in production control. He had been reassigned as part of the company's plan to reorganise the technical area. We were to discover that his redeployment was part of a much larger shift in the company's operations. It had opted to severely pare back its investment in research and development, which did not bode well for the future.

After non-stop pressure of union activity at work, suddenly I was able to think about wider politics. Along with millions of others I was sympathetic with the Campaign for Nuclear Disarmament (CND) aims and had attended a couple of CND's public meetings, one of them at my old school in Lockleaze. A revival of the anti-Nuclear movement had occurred in the late 1970s and early 1980s in response to the concern that a new generation of US nuclear weapons was to be placed in Britain and other Western European countries.[131] A reflection of its increasing influence on public opinion was Margaret Thatcher's appointment of Michael Heseltine as her new Secretary of State for Defence. She assigned him the task of counteracting the arguments put forward by CND.

Women became involved in the peace movement in large numbers and had a particularly significant impact. In September 1981 a small group of women established a peace camp outside RAF Greenham

Common Airbase, in Berkshire, using non-violent direct-action methods in an attempt to prevent the siting of cruise missiles there. The presence of these women 24 hours a day attracted great publicity and garnered support from thousands of women. The women's camp was to remain active for nineteen years.

On the 10th February 1983, the same day that 30 women peace campaigners were arrested in Downing Street for wilful obstruction,[132] I went to the theatre with Chris to see the anti-war play *When the Wind Blows* by Raymond Briggs. It demonstrated the absurdity of the government's *Protect and Survive* pamphlet advising what one should do in the event of a nuclear war. Chris's response was "can man really be so stupid?" Neither of us needed convincing but for anyone who doubted, Briggs conveyed a powerful anti-war message. I found the satirical scene, where the husband and wife characters blindly follow government instructions on building an inner refuge, both tragic and hilarious.

A few days later, I heard from the Open University that I was registered on its module *17th Century England: A Changing Culture*. My interest, which had been aroused at the WRP's Marxist Education College in 1978, had led me to read Christopher Hill's work, *The Century if Revolution 1603-1714* and I really wanted to gain a greater understanding. This was my chance.

* * *

While the tumult at work of the previous twelve months might have died down, before long the strains in my relationship with the management began to resurface. When difficulties arose in the working environment and training of staff using VDUs, managers failed to deal with the situation. Old habits of ignoring the problems faced by staff, and eschewing consultation with chapel officers, had reasserted themselves. I felt particularly apprehensive about three interim operating agreements that I had signed in mid-February: the computerisation of estimating the cost of production of orders, data input into the WIP store and material control computer systems. All three agreements had been set to run for three months, so any unforeseen problems could be located and tackled.

In mid-March, I wrote to the personnel manager saying that unless the concerns of staff using computer assisted systems were addressed I would not be willing to sign full operating agreements at the end of this three month trial period.[133] There was a flurry of activity. New ergonomic chairs arrived, and an order was placed for office computer desks. Training for a new telex machine (an electronic way of sending messages) was arranged and the questionnaires for the job evaluation system distributed to chapel members. By mid-May I was satisfied with the progress made and concluded a full agreement for the implementation of a computerised online estimating system to calculate selling prices and production times.

By this time, the disciplinary hearings with those members who had failed to comply with the SOGAT directive to strike on the 22nd September 'Day of Action', proved unfeasible and had to be abandoned. Moreover, it was strongly recommended that, in future, industrial action should only take place if it had been authorised by a ballot of the membership.[134] Some members had become bitter because they were denied a ballot. Also, several of my chapel members directed their hostility against me because I upheld the union's decision to support the health workers. It was difficult because I felt strongly that as everyone benefits from having a publicly run health service, a day's strike in support of NHS workers demanding an end to pitifully low pay rises was not much to ask. Moreover, I did not want SOGAT's authority to be weakened at a time when unions were under attack from an anti-union government. I found myself in alliance with my fellow branch committee member, Mike Vine. We both argued to continue with the hearings but due to their divisive impact, the majority of the branch committee overruled us.

Mike, who had been employed at St. Stephen's Press, worked as a bag tackler for DRG Packaging Bags, Bedminster. He was a member of the Communist Party and had been an active member of its factory branch in his previous job at St. Stephen's Press before it was taken into administration and closed in 1979. Despite our associations with opposing Trotskyist and Stalinist Communist parties—and holding allegiances to different Bristol football clubs—we worked closely together as trade union activists. Highly principled, committed and funny, Mike was someone who I could depend upon. We did not allow political differences to break the bond that had formed between us. When addressing me, sometimes he used the nickname, teasingly, of prof or professor because I was becoming rather studious.

I had begun my Open University (OU) module, at the end of March, often taking over the dining room table in the evenings after dinner. The course was interdisciplinary and covered the economy, education, science, politics, religion and the arts, providing insights into what life was like in the seventeenth century. The module was divided into nine blocks, released in stages over 32 weeks. There were set books to read, televised material to watch and radio programmes and cassette tapes to listen to. I had to produce nine assignments in essay form; a question on the contents covered in each block. I was daunted by the prospect of studying ten to fourteen hours a week and writing essays because that kind of academic commitment was an unknown quantity.

Applying myself to a cycle of learning like this proved to be even more difficult than I thought it would be. I was not after all simply a lone student. There was my daily life in a family. Together with Chris and the children, in mid-April I went to stay at a friend's caravan in Wareham, Dorset, where we celebrated Amanda's (my eldest daughter) fourteenth birthday. Three weeks later, Chris started a new demanding, but meaningful, job on days, as a care assistant at the Hostel for the Blind in Cotham, Bristol. Then of course there were my union commitments. In early May, I was at a weekend SOGAT South West and South Wales district meeting in Weston-super-Mare. On 21st May I travelled to Bournemouth as a delegate to the SOGAT policy conference, taking some of my OU course materials to work on in the evenings and forgoing some of the organised social events for delegates.

On the Tuesday afternoon conference session, backed by my chapel and the Bristol and West of England branch, I advocated from the podium that SOGAT 82 adopt a policy of withdrawing cooperation from the proposed Tory Youth Training Scheme (YTS), which planned to pay trainees a meagre fixed allowance of £25 per week. In its place I called on SOGAT to

> urge the TUC to expand its unemployment centres and organise their own training schemes for youth, which should also provide classes to educate youth in the principles of trade unionism and the history of struggle to win basic democratic rights.

I gave as an example a youth training centre operating in Brixton, which had been established by the Young Socialists wing of the WRP.

Mike, Amanda & Jacqueline Richardson, 1984/5.

A SOGAT member of an Area Manpower Board, the organisation appointed to administer the YTS, opposed my motion on the grounds that if the unions walk away from the Youth Training Scheme it would leave young people open to the influence of fascist movements. The National Executive Council was also opposed saying that they could not "find favour with any part of it." Thus, my motion was lost. Somewhat ironically, the next day Bill Keys, the joint General Secretary, called on all SOGAT members to oppose Tory policies which had done "so much damage to the economic-social fabric of the nation" and "unite together in working for the return of a Labour Government" in the forthcoming June general election.[135] It was one thing to talk in generalisations, but when it came to the specifics the options narrowed.

On my return to Bristol, I found the general election campaign in full swing. With my daughter Amanda I went to listen to Vanessa Redgrave's speech at South Street School in Bedminster in support of the local WRP candidate Linda Byrne (née Cheek). I was not involved in canvassing or crusading for Linda this time, but I was still associated with the All Trades Union Alliance, the industrial arm of the WRP. She trailed in last of six contestants with 113 votes, lower than she had recorded in 1979. The Conservatives, in a period when unemployment was hovering around the three million mark, trounced Labour by winning 397 seats to 209. The left within the Labour Party was also under pressure from the right. Tony Benn lost his seat in the newly created Bristol East constituency to the Conservative candidate, Jonathan Sayeed, by the thinnest of margins.

Despite WRP's feeble election result they picked up some recruits from Parkers Bakeries (part of the Sunblest group) in Cater Road, South Bristol (near my home in Withywood). This was a period when jobs in the catering industry were being cut at an alarming rate. The company was attempting to replace its six-day, eight-hour shift working with a 55-hour, 5-day week. A strike ensued. When the dispute petered out after a month or two the WRP south Bristol branch went into decline.

Though hugely disappointed I did not dwell on these political setbacks for both the revolutionary left and left reformism. I had immersed myself in studying historical events and experiences that I believed helped me to learn and understand the dynamics of capitalism and class struggle in Britain. Furthermore, I still had the responsibility of continuing to defend my members' interests at work.

At DRG FP, a welcome interval of relative tranquillity in management/union relations allowed the joint job evaluation panel to begin its work in assessing and grading the jobs of SOGAT clerical staff. Bob and I also carried out the three-month review of new technology agreements, which showed that apart from a few minor points they were working well. Thus, I was able to keep up with my OU studies, allowing me to have a stress-free summer break.

* * *

For our family vacation we stayed on a caravan site near the coastal town of Hastings where Robert Tressell (aka Noonan) the author of *The Ragged Trousered Philanthropists* had lived in the early 1900s. I had been reading the book and I liked the simplicity and humour in which he explained how capitalists easily duped workers and exploited them. One example of how workers' grim lives were "sometimes enlivened with a little innocent merriment" is given in Tressell's fictional account of the annual works' beano. His description of the rituals of employers' benevolence in 'treating' its employees to a day's outing, still apply. It reminded me of the commemoration of DRG FP's 50th anniversary in

DRG FP 50th Anniversary paperweight, 1978.

the grounds of an eighteenth century mansion house at Doddington Park (now the home and estate of the entrepreneur and inventor, James Dyson) south Gloucestershire, where the company staged a 'fun day' for all of its employees and their families. Every member of the workforce received an engraved Wedgewood glass paperweight in a presentation box, memorialising the special occasion. I have no knowledge of how much the event, which I did not attend, had cost the company, but I suspect it was cheaper than giving its employees a decent pay rise.

I was keen to explore Hastings, partly for traces of Tressell and also because many of the scenes in the novel were based on his experiences working there.

In the early 1980s the resort was in a rundown state. Its one-time flourishing fishing industry was in serious decline. Local people relied on tourist work and the public sector for jobs. Both were mainly low paid, and an air of depression pervaded the town. Nonetheless, I did find sites associated with Robert Tressell and his book such as 2 York

Buildings (near Hastings Castle), where he had tended a general builders and hardware store and used his artistic skills on hand painted signs. I was also curious about the history of the town, so we walked up to the castle, went to the museum and were intrigued by underground tunnels used by smugglers.

*　　*　　*

In late June I, along with the NGA FoC, John Price, received an invitation to rejoin the company's works council. The request strengthened my belief that the company was aiming to use the council as a forum to increase its managerial control. Though it liked to portray a harmonious relationship between managers and staff working together "to obtain a greater degree of success and achievement", behind this façade lurked the old management arrogance.[136] They persisted in their refusal to recognise that employees may not share the same set of objectives as the company. The agenda on the works council was primarily a propaganda platform for rolling out bland statements about how, in order for them to stay cost competitive, wage increases had to be matched by higher productivity. The council was never a platform for discussing pay, working conditions and job security because these were matters for negotiation simply between the unions and the company.

The clerical chapel had taken part in council meetings during 1981, but then had withdrawn, at my behest, in March 1982 and the NGA had pulled out around the same time. I had been a constant critic of the council since its inception in 1980. I wrote then to the factory FoCs arguing that the company had used it "to hammer home" its difficult financial position and convey the message that wages were too high, productivity too low, and employees far too inflexible. I went on to say that rather than "hoping to get some say in company policy" our duty was "to fight against management's attack on jobs, conditions of employment and living standards."[137] My view in September 1983 had not changed and with the clerical chapel's support I wrote to the joint secretary of the works council, Brian Wensley, rejecting the council's invitation, adding that trade unions were the only acceptable avenue for consulting with the workforce.[138]

That autumn the NGA confronted a more pressing affair. By October, a strike between the NGA and the owner of the Messenger Newspaper Group, Eddie Shah, which had begun on 4th July, was showing signs of escalating into a dispute that would prove to have wide implications for the trade union movement. It reached boiling point a month later, when the NGA mounted a three-day mass picket outside Shah's print works at Warrington in an attempt to stop the distribution of his weekly newspapers. NGA chapel officers from DRG FP, and some of their members, were among those on the picket line.[139]

On 17th November, the NGA was fined £50,000 for breaking an injunction, granted in mid-October, which had directed the union to stop hindering Shah and the Messenger Group from carrying out their business activities. The union refused to pay. At the end of the month, the High Court ordered the sequestration of union funds to pay fines of £150,000 for contempt.[140] In autumn, my daughter Amanda met a teenager from Liverpool who had been at the Warrington picket. When he came to our house, he described to me the severity of the policing, which left some pickets with head and leg injuries. I was appalled and in early December I called on the SOGAT Bristol and the West of England branch committee

> to unequivocally give full support to the NGA in the fight against the Tory Government, the courts, the police and the employers who are involved in a violent conspiracy to destroy the basic democratic rights of the working class and its trade unions…

I also urged the branch committee to hire a coach to take protesters to Warrington and, if the picketing continued, inform the NGA Bristol Branch of our resolutions and send them a donation of £1000. [141]

My fellow committee member and comrade, Mike Vine, despite having learned that he was to be made redundant along with several others at DRG Packaging Bags, staunchly supported my proposals. Mike's response increased my respect for him. However, other committee members were at best ambivalent about giving practical assistance to the NGA. There was a legacy of resentment and suspicion because in the past the craft pride of the printers had rankled with other trade unionists in printing. Moreover, the branch secretary, Joe Selway, who often held in his breast pocket a cotton handkerchief stamped with an image of Stalin, resisted giving them financial assistance. He advised that if the NGA requested our help it should be in the form of an interest free loan. He also said that he would only provide transport to Warrington if enough members demanded it. Consequently, lack of practical support left my proposal backing the NGA rather hollow.

As it happened it was all too late, anyway. For on the same day as our branch committee meeting, the NGA suspended mass picketing so that it could resume talks with Shah at the Advisory, Conciliation and Arbitration Service (ACAS) office in London. This coincided with the TUC declaring that its policy was backing the NGA *within the law*. It thus looked unlikely that mass picketing at Warrington would ever be resumed.

While obtaining support for action to defend attacks on union rights had proved extremely difficult, the branch committee was nevertheless prepared to assist political causes like opposing the privatisation of the NHS. I gained its backing for the Bristol Trades Council and Community Campaign against the privatisation of the NHS, along with a donation of £100 to help them with organisational costs.[142] The Trades Council was well aware of the sinister implications contained in the October 1983 Griffiths' report on the NHS. It signified a move towards placing some health services under the control of private companies (outsourcing).[143] However, none of us could have foreseen how the powers of trade unions would be further curtailed and the public sphere of social provision was going to be slowly but surely diminished.

1984

I became involved in the Bristol campaign in the defence of the NHS. During January and early February, along with a few Trades Council delegates and others, I went to the early meetings at Betty Underwood's house in Knowle West, a 1930s council estate in south Bristol, to plan a local campaign. A Communist Party member, a trade union activist and a women's rights campaigner, I later learned Betty had chaired the first session of the Women's Liberation Movement Conference at Skegness in 1971.[144] She was a key organiser in the Trades Council public appeal to defend the NHS. She knew how to collect support in the local communities. At our meeting she allocated places for us to cover in door-to-door petitioning to obtain signatures, in her local area, to demand that the government protect the NHS and stop the transfer of key public health services to the private sector. In contrast with my efforts to sell the WRPs publications in the 1970s, I had no trouble in collecting signatures from most of the people living in Knowle West.

The main difficulty was finding anyone in during the day.

We were being assailed on several fronts. My comrade, Mike Vine, who also lived in Knowle West, had recently been one of four SOGAT members who had been made redundant at DRG Packaging Bags. It looked like a political decision because it was handled in such a summary way and they had all been forced out against their will. I called for an immediate enquiry but in January the branch committee rejected my petition by ten votes to four. The branch officers claimed they had conducted an investigation, and that the FoCs and MoCs concerned had accepted its findings. The assistant branch secretary tried to appease me with the weak assurance that "Mike Vine was on top of the [branch] list for future vacancies."[145] I was outraged. After a period of unemployment, eventually he secured a job at the Bristol book printer and publisher, J. W. Arrowsmith.

By this point, without any doubt, the print unions were on the retreat. At the end of January, the NGA purged its contempt of court by halting mass picketing, paying High Court fines totalling £625,000, apologising and assuring the presiding judge at Manchester High Court that action in contempt of court would not happen again. The assault on unions by Thatcher and her government was unremitting. On 26th January, the Foreign Secretary, Sir Geoffrey Howe, announced to the House of Commons that trade union membership at Government Communications Head Quarters (GCHQ) in Cheltenham was to be banned. The basic right to belong to a trade union was removed in a stroke. I regarded this as draconian. As the deadline of 1st March approached for staff at GCHQ to relinquish their union membership, I circulated a petition in protest to my members relaying the view of the General Secretary of the TUC, Len Murray, that there was no legal basis for Thatcher's unprecedented action.[146]

Thatcher's aim was clear. She was determined to destroy the power of organised labour. The attack on GCHQ unions was just the start. The Conservative Party was seeking revenge for the 'who rules Britain' fight with the miners in 1974, which had resulted in Edward Heath's electoral defeat. The Conservatives turned to Margaret Thatcher to do the job by striking directly at the very heart of the trade union movement, the NUM, with a punishing programme of pit closures. The coal industry had been nationalised in 1947 when the National Coal Board (NCB) was given the task of running the industry on behalf of the government. Ironically, Thatcher was able to take advantage of having control over the industry. She appointed Ian MacGregor, the already well-known union buster, to head the NCB. He proceeded to administer cuts in the industry and thus decimate the union in a ruthless fashion.

The timing favoured the government's plan. Thatcher threw the gauntlet down during the spring. Arthur Scargill was left with little choice but to pick it up and commence the battle to save the industry on which the jobs of thousands of miners depended. Building on a series of local stoppages that had already begun, he launched a campaign to spread the strikes to pits across the country.

Wide scale industrial action began in early March after the announcement of the closure of Yorkshire's Cortonwood pit, ostensibly on financial grounds, and the notification of the closure of a further 20 pits with 20,000 job losses. The NCB's actions were an attack on miners' livelihoods, which went on to become one of the largest confrontations between workers and the state since the 1926 General Strike. Moreover, as Seumas Milne painstakingly revealed in his book, *The Enemy Within*, the state pulled out all the dirty tricks it could to destroy the NUM and its president, Arthur Scargill, in order to break the miners, the Praetorian guard of the working class.[147] The miners' strike came to overshadow all events in 1984.

I felt heartened by the miners' courageous stand and campaigned for their victory, though, understandably, most of our members at DRG FP were more concerned about the imminent threat to their jobs. In the first two days of March, DRG FP management delivered a series of presentations on 'the state of the business' to all of its employees. Then on the 9th March the company gathered all the FoCs and their deputies, along with branch and national officials, at the company's Abbotts Leigh training college. Because my deputy, Bob, was on holiday, Brian Brown stood in to take his place, even though his manager had berated him for agreeing to attend. I was exasperated at the begrudging attitude of departmental and junior managers, despite the managing director's emphasis on the importance of setting up local talks without delay.

At this assembly of union officials, DRG FP's higher management outlined the operational changes and agreements, which they insisted were required to convince the DRG Executive to invest in the future of its flexible packaging subsidiary. After a question and answer session, a timetable was set for further discussions at departmental level between chapel officers and production (and office) managers. The company's aim was to settle outstanding disputes and to identify areas of further consultation and negotiation so that it could develop a credible investment plan to present to the Group Executive. Without a substantial financial outlay, the long-term viability of DRG FP looked uncertain.

The morning after returning from Abbots Leigh, I went to see the production control manager, Chris Shinner, to arrange a meeting to consult and identify the unresolved concerns we had. He seemed surprised that we wanted to meet. Nonetheless he agreed and contacted Hugh Neate, head of accounts, to come too. Brian Brown accompanied me. I opened our talks by condemning the reprehensible behaviour of Brian's supervisor in questioning his attendance at the colloquium of union officers and DRG executives at Abbots Leigh.[148]

Shinner's response was mute, and he looked completely bewildered. He was evidently uncomfortable in his new job. As a chemist and paper technologist, he had no experience as a production manager. I moved on to summarise the outstanding matters that I felt needed to be resolved but looked to Hugh Neate for comment. I said that before I could agree to sign up to the proposed investment programme, I required more detail on the new clerical wages agreement and the endorsement of a new disciplinary procedure. Also, I needed to know the company's ongoing computerisation plans, and clarification concerning the 84/85 Christmas holiday shutdown.[149]

Hugh Neate disclosed that he envisaged a reduction in the numbers of staff employed as the use of computers increased, though he thought that it would be at least twelve months before their impact would become apparent. I learned little through this meeting. But I was gratified that because of the safeguards in the new technology agreement, the company would only be able to cut jobs through the routes of natural wastage and voluntary redundancy. I updated the chapel committee on these talks later the same day but warned that we must closely monitor the unfolding situation.

DRG FP's problems were not unique; other print companies in the area)were also experiencing a decline in demand and financial losses. Print chapels at Mardon, Son & Hall, part of the Imperial Tobacco Group, had agreed to accept their company survival plan. In May, Robert Maxwell, the chair and chief shareholder of the Purnell & Sons printing plant at Paulton near Bristol, threatened to close his works if the print unions refused to cooperate with him in making substantial cost savings in order to secure jobs and a £17.2 million investment in plant and machinery, including a new gravure printing machine and two web-offset presses.[150] All in all, the outlook for printing and packaging companies was looking increasingly dark.

Even though I could recognise that a former strong trade union base was under threat in printing, I believed that the miners' strike had the potential of developing into a General Strike, which could bring down the Thatcher government. Hopes that this might happen, along with the pleasing news that I had passed my Open University module, sustained my morale during this period. And, despite the fact that unions were so beleaguered, within weeks of the onset of the miners' strike, a community-based movement of support for miners and their families had sprung into being by collecting food. In Bristol, for instance, Bishopston Labour Party strategically placed its members outside the CRS shop next to Horfield Baptist church in Gloucester Road. Bristol West Labour Party coordinated solidarity and sustained support by twinning with Penrhiwceiber colliery in South Wales. This provided regular assistance to around 570 miners and their dependents.[151] Similarly forms of practical solidarity appeared all over Britain.

Former Labour MP Ron Thomas and Dawn Primarolo, who later would become a Labour MP for Bristol South, established a Bristol Miners' Support Group at the Transport and General Workers Union headquarters in central Bristol. Representatives from colliery lodges in South Wales, took up semi-permanent residence there. Tony Davies, secretary of the Merthyr Vale lodge, was one of them. I was one of the few SOGAT Bristol and West of England branch committee members collecting and channelling donations to the Bristol support group. Whenever I could make time, I dropped in to help out.

Through April and early May, I was fully engaged in the continuation of talks over the investment programme at DRG FP, which rested on the acceptance of a new survival plan. The differences between the unions and the company seemed to be insurmountable. Negotiations were adjourned and I was able to take a week's leave to attend the SOGAT biennial delegate conference in mid-May.

This would be no ordinary meeting, coming as it did ten weeks into the miners' strike. On Tuesday 15th May 1984, production chapels at *The Sun* newspaper blocked the printing of a picture of Arthur Scargill raising his right hand in what resembled a Nazi salute, under the strapline 'MINE FUHRER', which *The SUN* intended to run on its front page. Instead, it was replaced with a blank space and the momentous explanatory statement:

> Members of all The Sun (*sic*) production chapels refused to handle the Arthur Scargill picture and major headline on our lead story. The Sun (*sic*) has decided, reluctantly, to print the paper without either.[152]

Excitement buzzed around the conference hall when the news spread that print workers at *The Sun* had refused to print the image defaming Scargill.

On Wednesday morning, the president of SOGAT, Brenda Dean, with the agreement of the Delegate Council, invited the vice president of the South Wales NUM, Terry Thomas, and the miners' agent for Rhondda, Aberdare and Merthyr, Emlyn Jenkins, to join her on the platform to hear the debate on an emergency motion calling for full support to the NUM. They were welcomed with a standing ovation after which John Mitchell of the London machine branch moved the emergency resolution.

As well as a commitment to aiding the miners financially, and organising lorries to send food to the South Wales mining communities, the key clause in the motion urged SOGAT to resolve to "participate fully in Days of Action and other solidarity action in support of the miners, including strike[s]." Bob Gillespie, from the Scottish Group, pushed for a more militant response. Exclaiming that he was fed up with listening to such calls, he declared that as the miners had not won within three months then the labour movement should "vote with their feet and get on the street, on the picket lines, with the miners, every bloody one of them."[153] But this was defined simply as a 'view'. As it had not been introduced as an addendum, the primary motion stood, which the conference delegates passed unanimously. Hence no demand for a General Strike came from the SOGAT conference, just a rather tired request to the TUC to give "total and unstinting support for the NUM from all affiliated Unions".[154]

In the afternoon, both Terry Thomas and Emlyn Jenkins were called upon to address the conference. Terry spoke first. He opened by briefly tracing the background to the dispute, emphasising the devastating impact a piece of anti-union legislation, enacted in the 1980 Social Security Act and updated in 1983, had on miners' families.

This law required cutting supplementary benefit payments to strikers' dependents by £15 a week. The irony, that the families of miners jailed during the dispute were entitled to the £15, because their men were no longer classified as strikers, did not escape Terry. Up to 11th May he reported that 1,600 miners had been arrested. Charges ranged from distributing leaflets with the words of *Ode to a Scab* by the American socialist and novelist, Jack London,[155] to obstruction and assault. Terry finished his address by picking up Bob Gillespie's plea made in the morning session.

> [W]hen the time comes if it is necessary for a general strike in this country to prevent the attack on the trade union movement, we shall be prepared to go down that road as well.[156]

This was music to the ears of many delegates, including my own. The resolve of these miners' representatives was uplifting, despite all they had gone through, and I longed for them to repeat their victories of 1972 and 1974.

Returning back to my base in Bristol I resumed the tricky negotiations over the investment plan with a heightened impatience. Crucially, I managed to convince the company into withdrawing the detrimental changes it wanted to make to our computer agreement. In exchange, I pledged that our members would cover up to five non-union staff jobs that were expected to go over a three-year period, as a result of the introduction of new technology. Along with the engineering unions and the SOGAT Ink and Roller chapel, I was ready to sign an agreement, but the changes in working practices expected to lead to higher productivity required from other SOGAT chapels, and the NGA, were greater, so unsurprisingly they rejected it. Hence, the DRG Executive withdrew their support. Starved of funding, DRG FP's managing director, David Richards, made the ominous statement that the company "must now work to make a success of those parts of the business in which we have a future." This suggested that the company aimed to reduce its size, possibly by spinning off parts of its business as independent entities.[157]

At the clerical chapel AGM in early June, I was re-elected as FoC but Bob, my deputy, stood down because he was leaving to join the Technical, Administrative and Executive division of the union. Bob had been promoted to head the sales executive medical section. His

Gwen & Bob Brain, 1980s.

resignation left a huge void to fill, and I would come to miss his advice and support immensely. Fortunately, Gwen Cheetham, who would later become Bob's partner, volunteered to take over from him and she was duly elected. A feisty and principled woman, Gwen had proved her mettle both when she refused to give in to the bullying behaviour of her supervisor, and in carrying out her role as a chapel representative.

Another experienced union steward, Brian Brown, also declared that he no longer wished to serve as a chapel officer. Despite our differences, I recognised and acknowledged the ability he had shown in connecting with those chapel members who were either inactive or rarely expressed their opinions. New people joined the committee, but we were still one short and I was left to cover the health and safety position. At the end of the meeting, I passed a hat round for donations to support the miners and their families during their dispute. We collected £11.80 from the 26 members present to compliment the £10 we had already sent from our chapel funds to Emlyn Williams, the president of South Wales Area of the NUM.[158]

The following month, at the summer quarterly general meeting of the SOGAT Bristol and West of England branch, I seconded a motion moved by Mick Byrne, a print worker, and former member of the Socialist Labour League, demanding that SOGAT petition the TUC to call "a General Strike in support of the miners and to defeat [the] dictatorial and reactionary government." We argued that assistance in the form of food and finance, while important, was not enough to bring victory for the miners. "No section of workers fighting alone can win against the full force of the state, only the mobilisation of the whole working class by the TUC" could stop government plans to carry out wholesale pit closures.[159]

We were both aware of the role of the TUC in 1926 when, in backing the miners, it had supported a General Strike by bringing out key sections of the workforce, only to order them back to work just nine days later without securing any concessions from the Conservative government. However, we thought that if the TUC was pushed into leading a General Strike again, it would be difficult for it to abandon the miners a second time, and leave them to fight on alone, without losing all credibility. Our motion was passed with just two voting against; though I knew that our ostensible success came about from a poorly attended meeting. Unlike NATSOPA who had between 400 and 500 delegates at its meetings in the days prior to amalgamation, SOGAT rarely assembled more than 50. No doubt the presence of Tony Davies, lodge secretary of the Merthyr Vale Colliery, as a guest speaker at the meeting may well have garnered support for our motion from waverers, even though he did not put the miners' case until after the vote had been taken.

After Tony had thanked delegates for their support and updated them on the latest developments in the dispute, an emergency resolution was carried to donate a £1000 from the SOGAT Bristol and West of England branch to the South Wales Miners' fighting fund.

Following the collapse of the investment plan at DRG FP, my focus turned to the huge task of completing the job grading assessment of clerical and technical work under our union/management evaluation scheme. Over July and August most grades had been agreed, bar a couple of appeals, but a small minority of members had not completed their job description questionnaires. I appealed to them to inform their departmental union representative if there was a problem.

I found my involvement in the management and execution of the job evaluation scheme exceedingly burdensome and unrewarding. This was accentuated when the miners' strike reached a critical point. In early September, delegates to the TUC annual congress gathered in

Brighton to hear the TUC General Council's statement on the miners' dispute. The NUM put forward its motion demanding total support and a combination of the "mightiest mobilisation of power and strength of the movement at all levels."[160] When this resolution passed unanimously, it raised the hopes of striking miners, their families and their supporters. Then, several days later, the pit deputy's union, the National Association of Colliery Overmen, Deputies and Shotfirers (NACODS), decided to ballot its membership on an all-out strike. This too was more welcome news.

In late September, days before the result of the NACODS ballot was expected, I invited two miners' representatives to address the clerical chapel. I met them outside the factory ten minutes before the early evening meeting was due to start and smuggled them into the building. For obvious reasons, I had not asked the company permission for them to enter the premises, thus I had to act covertly. Only the chapel committee knew that they were coming. Quickly and quietly, I led them to the training room and introduced them to the chair, Janet St. George. She opened the meeting by welcoming them and said they would be speaking about their dispute after we had concluded our chapel business. Their presence triggered soft murmurings either of approval or unease, but no one openly complained.

My FoC's report stated that we had struck three new interim computer agreements in subdivisions of the accounts office. Several office sections were now using new technology, thus I felt we had reached a point where we had a strong case to push the company to concede a 35-hour week.

After I had finished my report, and other chapel matters had been dealt with, Janet turned to the NUM secretary of the Merthyr Vale lodge, Tony Davies, to put the miners' case in their dispute with the NCB and the Conservative government. I looked around and could sense that some members looked displeased to be put in the awkward position of whether to leave or stay to listen. Nobody left however, and Tony made an impassioned speech. During his talk I passed a hat round for donations; £15.51 was raised from the 34 members present for Tony to take back to the Bristol Miners' Support Group. We paid Tony and his colleague's travel expenses out of chapel funds.[161]

Two days later NACODs announced an 82.5 per cent vote in favour of strike action, but its executive wanted talks with the NCB under the auspices of the Advisory, Conciliation and Arbitration Service (ACAS) before implementing the will of its members. Pressure intensified when the print production workers, members of the NGA, SOGAT and the Electrical, Electronic, Telecommunications and Plumbing Union (EETPU), at *The SUN* Newspaper walked out when management refused to withdraw a front page editorial describing miners as the "scum of the earth". *The SUN* also failed to appear on Monday 1st and Tuesday 2nd October because management refused to meet the print workers' demand for payment for Saturday's paper.[162]

On 12th October, just after talks between the NUM, NACODS and the NCB, under the auspices of ACAS, had begun, five people were killed when a bomb, planted by the Irish Republican Army (IRA), exploded at the Grand Hotel, Brighton, during the Conservative Party Conference. Margaret Thatcher, who was staying at the hotel, escaped unhurt. As a consequence of the bombing, she toned down the conference speech that she had intended to deliver. Remnants of the original draft survive. It reveals that the dominant message she had wanted to get across was that 'the enemy within', the striking miners and their supporters across all sections of the Labour Party, were the ones who posed the greatest threat to democracy.[163]

This speech was never delivered. Notably, her attacks on the Labour Party concerning the miners' strike were removed. Instead, she narrowed the focus of her speech to the threat of 'the emergence of an organised revolutionary minority ...prepared to exploit industrial disputes, but whose real aim is the breakdown of law and order and the destruction of democratic parliamentary government.'[164]

Four days after the Brighton bombing, ACAS talks between the NUM, NACODS and the NCB broke down. NACODS announced that it would call out their members on 25 October. At the last minute, however, it called off the strike. Reneging on an agreed joint position it had had with the NUM, "it put forward a proposal for an 'independent' non-binding element within the colliery review procedure" that was unacceptable to the NUM.[165] The chance of the miners achieving a historic victory was removed at a stroke of a pen. Betrayal was on the lips of striking miners. The prospect of them being defeated was devastating and I realised that any hope of securing solidarity industrial action from other unions in aiding the miners' struggle had finally ended.

So, from November we concentrated on collecting and distributing food, largely through support groups, and fund raising. At the SOGAT Bristol and West of England branch committee meeting in early

November I gave a report on the work of the Bristol miners' support group, stressing its importance in sustaining miners' families and keeping up their morale.[166] I also ordered ten pamphlets of *The Miners' Case* for distribution to my chapel members to provide them with an alternative view from what they may have read in the tabloid press.

While my chapel committee was prepared to support striking miners, the Bristol and West of England full time officers were equivocal. In November the NGA proposed a joint rally with the SOGAT branch in aid of the miners. The new branch secretary, Bernard Vowles, denied the branch committee a chance to discuss this suggestion by pre-emptively sending the NGA a letter of rejection. I, and a few others, protested at this disrespect towards the committee, but to no avail. Nonetheless, my appeal to donate £250 to the Bristol Miners' Support Group was carried.[167]

As Christmas approached, food collections and fund raising intensified, including the selling of raffle tickets and mementoes. London print workers sold commemorative Christmas mugs, the proceeds of which went to the Striking Miners' Children Appeal Support Fund. Some of these were sold to SOGAT members in Bristol and I still have the one I bought all those years ago. SOGAT London Central and Machine branches also contributed 2,000 turkeys and arranged Christmas parties for children in many mining communities.[168]

For some trade union critics of the strike, its long duration, the onset of Christmas and the hardships endured by miners' families, brought about a more benevolent view. I was heartened when Alan Clarke, a union representative for the Banking, Insurance and Finance Union (BIFU), and a Green Party member, circulated a Christmas card to send to the miners from Grendel chess club members, which I signed. Alan said at the beginning of the strike he had been quite unsympathetic towards the NUM leadership because it refused to hold a national ballot. Eventually, however, his "sympathies towards the miners themselves prevailed."[169]

He was part of a great swathe of supporters throughout the country. The miners' strike had an extraordinary impact on many people, which was both personal and political.

1985

The equivocal support the miners received from the TUC and Labour leaders, which effectively ruled out any hope of 'official' wider assistance through secondary industrial action, seriously weakened them in their struggle against the NCB and the government. The prospect of defeat began to loom as morale faltered. The sense of desperate urgency I experienced at the time is evident in the resolution I moved at a clerical chapel meeting in mid-January.

> This DRG FP clerical chapel calls upon the Bristol & West of England Branch to urge the NEC to ensure that SOGAT 82 retains its complete independence from the state and that it takes this policy vehemently into the TUC.

Though SOGAT 82 did not accept government money for ballots and denounced labour movement figures from accepting any state honours, the motion explicitly mentioned

> the peerages bestowed upon Len Murray, former TUC General Secretary and Frank Chapple, former EEPTU General Secretary [and] the acceptance of government money by the EEPTU for ballots. It is therefore imperative that SOGAT 82 fights within the TUC for the complete and unconditional independence of the trade unions in relation to the state.

The motion went on to highlight the "catastrophic results" of adopting a collaborative approach to the state, "the banning of unions at GCHQ and the fines imposed on the NGA, NUM & TGWU." Adding that it had been left to "the valiant struggle of the miners" to halt "this onslaught." I predicted "if they lose a tidal wave of destruction will fall upon the union movement and ITS MEMBERS (*sic*)."[170]

To my relief, the resolution was carried, and after some resistance from the Bristol and West of England branch secretary, I was allowed to move it at the branch general meeting on 21st January. It passed with no opposition,[171] though, in reality, it was a pyrrhic victory for motions did little for the chances of an NUM victory. It does, however, indicate the overwhelming dismay I felt about being so powerless. I was desperate to alleviate the ominous sense of impending defeat. Perhaps all those who voted for it shared a similar apprehension of the fatal significance of this conflict.

Twelve months had passed since the conflict had broken out at GCHQ. I knew this was a really significant struggle. At the end of the January clerical chapel meeting, I appealed to my members to join me, and others, at Cheltenham for the GCHQ one-year anniversary march in protest against the denial of the right to belong to a trade union. The chances of persuading the government to make a U-turn were slim, but I was convinced of the need to keep on resisting against the injustices of the state. SOGAT, like many other unions, had organised coach travel from Bristol. Although only a few from my chapel attended, the coach was reasonably full of other SOGAT members from across Bristol. I was one of seven who volunteered to carry the SOGAT Bristol and West of England branch banner. It felt good to be part of a sizeable local movement. Nevertheless, Margaret Thatcher's second term of office was a dark time for trade union rights.

Back at DRG FP rumours were circulating that the company was about to be taken over. The increase in its share price reflected investors' confidence in the company's prospects in the expectation that this would happen.[172] Management at DRG FP, however, continued to dismiss reports that DRG was in danger of being appropriated as mere paper talk. It used the works council as a platform to quash what it saw as hearsay and it was trawling energetically for representatives from all sections of the workforce to put over its version of what was happening to the business. When the management asked me to reconsider lifting the clerical chapel boycott of the council,[173] I refused. At a convention of the DRG FP SOGAT Council (an in-house combine committee of all SOGAT chapels) I reiterated the reasons I had given to the NATSOPA Council in 1980.[174]

More importantly, during this meeting I proposed that SOGAT should petition for a new clause to be added to the New Technology agreement. I had been following health and safety reports on the high incidence of miscarriages among young women using VDUs.[175] So I argued that if a woman VDU operator was confirmed pregnant, she should be relieved of this work and moved to take on non-VDU tasks until the birth and return to work. As chair of the SOGAT council I was designated to take this up with the company. It met resistance and I wrote to Bernard Vowles, the SOGAT Bristol and West of England branch secretary, asking him to pursue it on our behalf.[176] The best he could achieve was a commitment from the personnel manager, Arthur Alletson, that the company was "prepared to treat with sympathy and understanding a request from any pregnant employee to be moved from a job entailing the operation of a VDU to some other work not involving the use of a screen".[177] This, of course, put the onus on the individual worker.

In this period, a disagreement over the interpretation and application of the job evaluation scheme arose. I had complained because Chris Shinner had intervened to prevent the implementation of a job evaluation panel assessment. Shinner challenged the assessment on the grounds that the panel was divided. However, this ran counter to the agreed evaluation procedure, which stated that when an evaluation was not achieved in common that "an average will be calculated". The proviso was that all members of the Panel would accept this.[178] On this occasion panel members had endorsed the average score. But under pressure from Shinner, the company changed its mind and decided to re-evaluate the original decision. I made it clear that this was unacceptable. Only when I threatened to invoke the disputes procedure did the company accede to implementing the panel's original assessment.[179]

Personally, I was relieved that we did not have to pursue the matter. The evaluation process was difficult to encapsulate in a hard and fast manner as circumstances varied. I had never been comfortable with the abstract character of the evaluation scheme and I was exceedingly glad to hand over my place on the panel, in May, to Bob Palmer, the chapel representative for sales and production control. Having dropped one of my union duties, I reluctantly took on another.

After repeated requests from Arthur Alletson, the chapel committee agreed that Gwen, my deputy, and I should present ourselves at the June works council meeting as observers. Just a few days before we were due to make our guest appearance the company issued compulsory redundancy notices on eight NGA members. I hastily wrote to Alletson saying "the Chapel Committee feel that, until the picture clarifies, it will be inappropriate to show any form of support for the Works Council".[180] Consequently we refused to attend. Unfortunately, other SOGAT chapels did not adopt the same approach.

At the council meeting the company avoided the subject of redundancies on the grounds that "it would be unfair to talk [about NGA redundancies] when the NGA [was] not represented." It went on to say that "if there were to be any significant number of redundancies

Mike Richardson, 1985, speaking at Castle Green, Bristol, supporting the call to release the jailed miners.

the Works Council would be told in advance."[181] Although I did not realise it at the time this was a subtle forewarning of what was to come.

* * *

At the beginning of June, the youth section of the WRP, the Young Socialists, organised marches from Scotland, Liverpool and Swansea demanding the release of the jailed miners and reinstatement of those who had been sacked. When the Swansea contingent stopped in Bristol on Saturday 22nd June it held an open-air rally on Castle Green, near the shopping centre in Bristol. I went along and was called on to speak in a personal capacity. I was a peripheral supporter, and this was not pre-arranged, and thus I was caught by surprise. But it was good seeing the resolve and zeal of all these young people. I took the microphone, stepped onto a low wall and began with the words: "I salute the tenacity and the vitality of the comrades on this march and I also salute its aims." I went on somewhat optimistically to declare, "The march is a reflection of the whole working class and its will to fight…"[182]

The whole working class might not have been listening but one, a young woman chapel member, Alison Stallard, was. On the following Monday she came and told me she had been in the city on Saturday and heard me address the young socialists and their supporters at the rally. It was satisfying to know that the message 'free the jailed miners' had reached someone out browsing and buying in Bristol's stores. I knew Alison's father, a SOGAT member. He was employed in the work-in-progress store. The previous year when a vacancy had come up for a junior office worker, I had suggested to him that his daughter should apply. The long tradition of familial recruitment at DRG FP continued, despite the dramatic fall in numbers employed from around 1800 in 1970 to about 800 in 1985. This could combine with a commitment to union membership. Paradoxically, it was actually the strength of union representation that then contributed to a sense of real connection to the work we were doing.

* * *

In late April, Stafford, a county town in the west midlands, suffered a large outbreak of Legionella's disease. Of the 68 confirmed cases 22 died. Legionella bacteria were traced to the cooling tower of the air conditioning system at the town's district general hospital. This alerted health officials throughout the country where cooling towers were in use, particularly in hospitals but also factories and large office blocks. At Nuffield's Chesterfield Hospital in Bristol, tests revealed Legionella bacteria in a hot tap in a nurses' changing room. The hospital closed for ten days while the water system was cleaned.[183]

In June, when it came to light that a DRG FP employee in hospital was thought to have Legionnaires' disease, SOGAT FoCs pushed for an enquiry. On 2nd July, in my role as chair of the SOGAT Council, I wrote to Arthur Alletson enclosing an article on Legionnaires' disease in a Sunday magazine, which contained some information that cast doubt on the adequacy of the facts the company had recently issued to FoCs. The disease is contracted through the Legionella bacterium, that can multiply and thrive in a building's water system to spread in small water droplets in the air, which people can inhale. Shower heads, if not cleaned regularly, are another source in which the bacterium can grow.

Given this 'new' evidence I requested that a date for an enquiry should be established.[184] The company's position was that it had acted upon the advice of the water treatment company, Thermochem, checking water systems and humidifiers regularly, and dosing "the water with the appropriate chemicals".[185] At the July works council the company agreed that it would set up an enquiry saying that "there had not been any attempts at a cover up" and that "current water tests were giving a negative result and it was the job of the people conducting the enquiry to establish the facts through a totally open route."[186]

The enquiry team consisted of the factory FoCs, including me, and was headed by Ken Mortimore, a senior member of the production technology laboratory, with whom I had frequent dealings in my work as a production scheduler. He was popular, very good at his job and unafraid of criticising people in authority on matters that related to his area of expertise.

We began our enquiry in September with a site check of the factory's cooling system and went on to have several meetings before submitting a final report. As a result of our findings the company clarified and confirmed with Thermochem's water analysis laboratory how to detect legionella bacteria in a water sample. In-house, the temperature of all hot water holding tanks, as advised by the Environmental Health Department (EHD), had to be kept at 60 degrees centigrade. Moreover, all shower heads had to be removed and disinfected every three months. Blood tests taken from a random group of workers were found to be negative and the company was advised by EHD that no more tests would be necessary.[187] The employee who contracted Legionnaire's disease survived but never fully recovered.

While the print unions were at one in handling health and safety concerns, such as water borne diseases, demarcation squabbles and conflicts between the unions persisted. In an attempt at conciliation, the Bristol Trades Council officers convened a meeting of the print union Council delegates to seek ways in which it could assist in bringing about a more cooperative relationship between the NGA, SOGAT and the National Union of Journalists (NUJ). As a result, in August the Council wrote to the Bristol branch secretaries of these unions to get their backing for the establishment of a local standing committee for the printing and media industry. Despite my plea to support the Council's initiative, the SOGAT branch committee rebuffed the idea and the enterprise collapsed.[188]

Also, during this time, I wrote to the managing director, Geoff Barnes, complaining about the lack of response to the backlog of outstanding disputes that the clerical chapel had with the company. To give it some weight, I sent copies to the DRG general manager of employee relations, Geoff Haigh, and the SOGAT Bristol and West of England branch secretary, Bernard Vowles. I emphasised that by disregarding the concerns of the clerical chapel, the company was taking a similar path to the one that led the chapel to take industrial action in 1982. I referred to a letter I had sent a few weeks prior to that action. It said that unless agreements were honoured, and meaningful dialogue and negotiations then took place, "we will be in constant conflict". I asserted these words were just as relevant to the situation in 1985 as they had been in 1982.[189]

This brought about an immediate response. Over the following weeks I was involved in a series of talks with Arthur Alletson to press the company to fill the vacancy for a trainee in the post room, deal with the assessments and appeals outstanding under the job evaluation scheme, and to respond to the clerical chapel's claim for a 35 hour week. On one occasion, in a break in our proceedings, I recall discussing John Steinbeck's novel, *The Grapes of Wrath* with him. I remember him saying that when he first read it the descriptions of the struggles and hardships endured by families heading for California during the Great Depression had moved him. His empathy seemed genuine, but he saw no connection to the Bristol workplace. His feelings did not transfer to our dealings. I could not understand how managers could make this kind of separation.

Our conversation about Steinbeck took place a week or so before Chris and I went to the Little Theatre in Bristol to see *The Ragged-Trousered Philanthropists* based on Robert Tressell's book. In my favourite scene, *The Great Money-Trick*, the principal character, Frank Owen, shows his fellow workers how the capitalist class was able to exploit the working class by deception. He does this dramatically by inducing them to take part in a scene in which he takes the role of the capitalist class while his associates act out the condition of the working class. The scene caught in a nutshell of comedy Karl Marx's labour theory of value.

I had responded powerfully to Tressell's irony, but I had also connected with the circumstances he depicted. This had been confirmed through contact with the WRP in the 1970s. I had begun to read Marx's and Engels' writings. During the 1980s I had withdrawn to its fringes only to be pulled back because an internal dispute had led to the organisation imploding. In October 1985, the WRP expelled its former leader, Gerry Healy, for alleged "repeated assaults on women members of the party".[190] This news sent the various factions in the party spinning in confusion. Members, along with former party members like me, gathered at meetings around the country to condemn Healy, some speaking of their own experiences of his abusive behaviour. I was invited to one of these in Bristol. I had never actually met Healy in person, though in the late 1970s I had been present at a large meeting at which he had ridiculed Vanessa Redgrave after she had spoken in a debate. In criticising her contribution, he had belittled her in an extremely unpleasant and bullying manner, which I found shameful.

Her brother, Corin Redgrave, who was a staunch Healy supporter, got wind of the meeting in Bristol and came to the city, resolved to gain entry. This would have made it difficult for people to speak freely. News of his arrival at Temple Meads railway station became known almost as soon as he had stepped off the train. I was in the delegation that left our meeting and confronted him and his escort as he was making his way on foot from the station to the meeting in Totterdown, south Bristol. After a long and acrimonious exchange of words he retreated. I watched in relief as he disappeared into the evening darkness and made his way back to whence he came. Some lapsed members went on to join other Trotskyist groups, others withdrew from active politics.

At work, I had to face more difficult matters. The talks about settling the clerical chapel's outstanding claims and complaints had stalled. I received just one letter from Alletson saying that the company was "not prepared to discuss" our petition for a 35 hour week.[191] More disturbingly, at 4pm on 26th November, one of my members, the artists' clerk, Mike Symonds, was abruptly given notice of redundancy. He was not afforded the opportunity of union representation. I was informed at the same time as Mike, but at a separate meeting at which, despite my protests, the company insisted on upholding its decision. Later it came to light the company had been covertly planning to sack Mike. Apparently, some members of his department knew of his impending fate three weeks before he did.[192]

I called on the assistance of a Branch officer. On 28th November we went together to negotiate with the company, but the only concession it offered was the possibility of substituting Mike with another clerical chapel member if a volunteer could be found. Later that day I reported the situation at an emergency chapel meeting. Predictably no volunteers to substitute for Mike came forward. The chapel agreed to impose an overtime ban. The SOGAT machine chapel suggested that one of their members volunteer as a substitute so that Mike could take up a position on the shop floor. I put this proposal to management who agreed to consider it.

1986

On 22nd January, the company's managing director, Geoff Barnes, wrote to DRG FP's employees giving notice that the company was cutting its 762 strong workforce by 95 due to the "excessive numbers" employed "coupled with the inflexibility in certain areas." He went on to say that any

> of our joint Agreements with Unions which do not contribute to the good of the business, and in many cases damage the effectiveness of the Company, will have to cease or be changed....

The SOGAT's new technology agreement was one of several examples that he inferred the company would terminate.

> The restrictions of the "Computer Agreement" on administration procedures adds further stress to an unwieldy administration system....
>
> Too much time and effort is required on industrial relation matters and not enough on the important issue of concentrating resource on items such as Customer needs, output, quality and beating the competition...[193]

The next day, redundancy notices were handed to ten office staff, including Mike Symonds, with a leaving date of the end of February. Except perhaps for Mike's post, none of the other jobs were dispensable.

They all needed someone to carry out the work. To achieve this, I knew that the remaining clerical staff would be expected to take on heavier workloads and accept plans to computerise more work without job security guarantees. The factory chapels did not face the same immediacy of compulsory redundancies that the clerical chapel did. The company figured that the clerical chapel would be the hardest nut to crack, believing that resolving the concerns of the SOGAT machine and finishing chapels would not be as difficult.[194]

On Monday morning, 27th January, office staff learned they were expected to absorb the work of those who were being made redundant. Senior managers informed them of the additions to, and changes in, their job specifications. Liz Griffiths, a new personnel assistant, informed me that my job would be reorganised within the scheduling section. This shuffle of scheduling responsibilities enabled management to transfer a non-union person to the section after a chapel member, Graham White, the flexographic scheduler, left the company upon learning that he was to be made redundant. Brian Brown was the only other person in production control who had been nominated to leave. His work was due to be shared among the remaining staff on the material control section.[195]

I was feeling the strain of years of constant conflict, battling against powerful forces in upholding my social and political principles that I believed served to advance the interests of my members. But the people identified to leave were in turmoil. I knew I had to try and get control of the situation. With the company's permission, I convened a full chapel meeting in the afternoon. Fifty-seven members assembled to hear my proposal on how we should respond to the company's unforgiving imposition of job cuts. I began with an attack on the business ethics of the company. I accused it of using fear tactics to try and make us conform. It wanted us to accept that redundancies were inevitable and to acquiesce to the termination of union agreements. I concluded by affirming what to me was obvious, that if there were "no effective union agreements" then there would be "no effective union representation". This I said must be resisted.[196]

Forty-eight out of the 57 members present backed my motion to call on the SOGAT Bristol and the West of England Branch and the National Executive Council to support a clerical chapel membership ballot to take industrial action if the company did not step down from its attempt to impose compulsory redundancies.[197] I took this bureaucratic and legal course despite its laboriousness, remembering the bad experience in 1982 when I had tried to secure backing for the low paid NHS workers.

However, the situation was changing rapidly. It came to light that Mike Symonds notice of leave for the end of February was inexplicably brought forward to the end of January. I had not been prepared for such a direct challenge to the decision we had made at the chapel meeting. I quickly changed tack because I saw that the only chance of forcing the company to retract or moderate its decision was to take immediate action rather than wait to see if we would get official backing from SOGAT. So, on 29th January, in order to bring the matter to a head, I directed two of my members, the chair of the chapel and switchboard operator, Janet St. George, and her co-operator, Pam Bromwich, to withdraw their labour in protest against the company's hostile action.

After two requests to work normally they were suspended that afternoon without pay for being in breach of contract. Their action, however, brought immediate results. I called on the assistance of a SOGAT branch area organiser, Len Stephen, who obtained some respite by securing a two-week delay in Mike's dismissal during which time the company promised to try and find suitable alternative work, on condition that he stay at home (on full pay). On this basis Len Stephen agreed that our two suspended members would resume normal working.

Nevertheless, the uncertainty was beginning to tell. Immediately after this dramatic intervention, Gwen, my deputy, informed me that she wanted to be considered for voluntary redundancy. Members began to approach me individually to discuss their particular situations, rather than their area representatives, which resulted in two more people volunteering to go.

This attack on us at DRG FP coincided with the large-scale dismissal of 5,500 print workers employed by Rupert Murdoch, the head of News International, on his publications *The Sun, News of the World, The Times* and *Sunday Times*. Like DRG FP, "News International considered 'overmanning', high wages, lightning strikes and opposition to technological change evils that could no longer be tolerated."[198] Murdoch relocated the printing of News International's newspapers to his new plant at Wapping without union representation by SOGAT and the NGA.

The outbreak of these disputes, and others that quickly followed, placed SOGAT at the forefront of the fight against ruthless employers who took advantage of legislation introduced in 1982 and 84, to curtail trade union immunities and outlaw secondary solidarity action, to impose radical changes detrimental to job security, pay and conditions. Bristol and the West Country workers were not excluded from this onslaught.

By the second week of February, it had become apparent that DRG FP had no intention of offering Mike Symonds alternative work. Although he was interviewed for several job vacancies by DRG subsidiary firms in the Bristol district, none offered him a post. In one intimidating interview, Mike said he felt he was capable of all the work duties that would be required of him, including "the over emphasis on toilet cleaning".[199] He was turned down for this job because he lacked ambition and drive! Therefore, on 11th February, a few days before he was due to leave, I assembled chapel members to debate and decide our response to Mike's pending dismissal and the company's intention to force through changes in working practices. In the latter case, the chapel voted by 28 to 23 to accept four of the six changes demanded by the company. Two of the changes were not put to the vote, the new technology agreement and rearranged working hours. Earlier in the day the company had issued termination notices on these agreements and I decided that we should oppose these pronouncements through the disputes procedure.

The signs were ominous when I came to make the case for an immediate strike on the grounds of our opposition to compulsory redundancies. There was one key factor in play; the company had already issued redundancy notices to the individuals concerned. Therefore, around 80% of the chapel probably felt that their jobs were secure, at least in the short term. I think this influenced the chapel's reversal of its previous decision to accept my proposal for an immediate strike by 27 votes to 24. Mike Symonds was not present, so this relieved any embarrassment members may have had in facing him. The impact of this on the chapel committee and me was devastating. As the members dispersed to return to their workplaces, in a fit of pique we agreed to resign at the next quarterly meeting.[200]

A mix of emotions overwhelmed me. I felt dejected, angry and sad all at the same time. They blended in a painful discord that was profoundly draining of energy and hope. Yet, I had to pick myself up for a meeting that evening to help organise a rota for picketing the newspaper distribution centre, W. H. Smith at Temple Meads, in support of the sacked News International print workers. Chris was unhappy about me being out again and was beginning to wonder if I knew that she existed.[201] I could not relax. When I stopped and pondered over the events of the previous few days, I felt troubled. Was I too hasty? Could I have done something different? I doubted my self-worth.

Unsurprisingly, by the next day management had already learned what had happened at our chapel meeting. Gwen and I met with management representatives and stuck to the line that SOGAT did not accept compulsory redundancies but said we were prepared to make some of the changes in working practices the company had demanded. We were wasting our breath of course.

While we were trying to salvage something out of a desperate situation, managers were already busy reallocating and rearranging our members' jobs. They were turning the screw. On returning to my office, I learned that instead of my work being reorganised within the scheduling section, I had now been allocated to take over Brian Brown's material control job on the 17th February. By taking the job of one of my members who had been made forcibly redundant I would have lost all my self-respect. Neither of our jobs was unnecessary; the work still required someone to do it. However, Arthur Alletson made it clear that if I refused to move on Monday the 17th I would be dismissed. I reminded him that as an elected SOGAT FoC I was entitled to be represented by a full-time SOGAT official.

On Sunday morning (1.30am to 4.30am), the day before I was due to be dismissed, I joined the picketing at W. H. Smith's distribution centre at Temple Meads along with other SOGAT members and their supporters. Among them were my closest comrade, Mike Vine, my old acquaintance, Andy Pickford, and a few other branch committee members. Dawn Primarolo also came to picket. She was an NGA member before becoming the Labour MP for Bristol South. The police kept us back as we barracked the drivers delivering the *News of the World* and *The Sunday Times* to W. H. Smith. There were some minor scuffles, and one van ran over a policeman's foot, but he was not badly hurt.

On Monday I was told that I would be expected to take over Brian Brown's material control job the following morning. I repeated that I would not move to take the job of an employee who had been made redundant against his will. I was then warned that I could be subject to instant dismissal indicating that my refusal would be regarded as an act of gross misconduct. I made arrangements to bring in a full-time SOGAT official to represent me.

On Tuesday morning my manager ordered me to move into and undertake Brian Brown's material control job. I refused. I was called to the personnel office and told to bring my union representative, the SOGAT area organiser, Len Stephen, who was waiting in reception. When we entered the office Jim Shaw, the company's production director, was standing by ready to invoke stage two of the company's disciplinary procedure. I gave my reason for refusing to conform. I reiterated that SOGAT's policy was to oppose compulsory redundancies and if I agreed to take possession of Brian's work, I would be assisting the company in unscrupulous manoeuvrings. Len registered a failure to agree under the disputes and grievance procedure, but the production director insisted this was purely a disciplinary matter. If I failed to obey a manager's instruction I would be discharged.

On Wednesday morning, the 19th February, I woke up with a shocking cold, not the ideal condition when facing dismissal. Soon after I arrived at the office, I was formally instructed to move to the material control section and begin training. I refused. I was given fifteen minutes to reconsider my decision. I was approached a second time and asked if I had changed my mind. I shook my head and turned away. I was warned that I would be dismissed if I did not comply. Later in the morning I received a letter confirming that I had been suspended with pay until 8am the next day to allow me more time to re-evaluate my position.[202]

In the afternoon, all the SOGAT FoCs (my deputy, Gwen Cheetham, acted on behalf of the clerical chapel) employed by the DRG group in the Bristol and South Western district gathered at the SOGAT branch office in Brislington. After a full discussion they sent out a call to their members to "stand together", from 6am Thursday, and refuse to cooperate with management in protest at my suspension. Moreover, the SOGAT FoCs broke off talks with the company and returned to work on their appropriate shifts.[203]

On Thursday morning, I was called to the personnel office, accompanied by Gwen, where I was given a final opportunity to relent. Again, I refused. Then I was presented with a letter stating that I was "dismissed without notice from the Company's employment with immediate effect."[204] Stuart Clack, with whom I had worked since the early 1970s, was given the task of accompanying me to the production control office, where he stood by while I picked up my personal belongings. Then, showing signs of unease, he escorted me off the premises. I arrived home and told Chris who had already been forewarned. She was fully

Production Control Office, 1990s.

supportive, though not so happy when I told her that I was on picket duty that night, especially as I was still suffering from a bad cold.

SOGAT chapels broke off talks with the company and on Friday afternoon, as a result of the non-cooperation policy, two members of the machine chapel were suspended for refusing to accept changes in their working practices. "The whole shift stopped work in support of their colleagues despite various threats by supervisors and managers."[205] On the weekend, I sent a letter to Geoff Barnes, DRG FP's managing director, appealing against my dismissal and requesting that I have a full-time union official at the hearing.[206]

The SOGAT machine chapel resumed work on Monday 24th February but continued with its non-cooperation policy. On the night shift, 10pm to 6am, the company suspended another member of the chapel for refusing to transfer from his current job to another one, on a glue-laminating machine, which led to a further stoppage. Work resumed at 6am Wednesday to enable talks with a SOGAT branch official to commence in an effort to resolve the problem.[207]

During this time, on Tuesday 25th, my appeal against unfair dismissal took place. Chris had bought me a second-hand black jacket the previous week, so I decided to wear it for the hearing. I pinned a SOGAT badge onto the lapel and after slipping on my coat, I put on a SOGAT tie for good measure.

Len Stephen, the full time SOGAT officer, and Brian Hopton, the SOGAT Bristol and the West of England assistant branch secretary, represented me. Geoff Barnes and Jim Shaw were on the other side of the table. The matters of disagreement were aired once again, after which Len raised for the first time that he believed I had been dismissed because of my trade union activities. Barnes strenuously denied this, but Len highlighted that two other members of the clerical chapel had refused to transfer to other jobs, but no disciplinary action had been taken against them. Barnes sidestepped the accusation stating that their cases were slightly different and that it was not necessary for the company to make them move. Unsurprisingly the hearing was a charade. The company upheld its decision.[208]

This was not the end of the affair. Members of the SOGAT finishing chapel struck work three days later in protest against the suspension of five of their members for carrying out their chapel's non-co-operation policy—a policy that came about as a result of both my suspension and dismissal—by "refusing to adopt new manning levels and changes in working practices that had not been negotiated." Four hundred and forty-eight of SOGAT's 450 shop floor members immediately downed tools and threatened to spread the dispute to other DRG companies.[209]

On Sunday 2nd March, SOGAT members within the DRG Bristol based group of companies met, endorsed the ongoing strike at DRG FP, and "pledged to join this fight as and when our own agreements and conditions are attacked." They agreed to adopt "a policy of working to agreements and the SOGAT rule book" in order to "nip this dispute in the bud".[210]

Buoyed by having received this support, the SOGAT machine and finishing chapels continued with their strike on Monday. On the same day the SOGAT Bristol and the West of England branch committee convened and ratified a resolution backing the action taken by the DRG chapels to secure the reinstatement of *all* of their sacked members.[211] Later, at 5pm, the clerical chapel assembled and, by 21 votes to 15, with 5 abstentions, approved a motion to join the SOGAT factory chapels' strike the following morning, at 8am.

Simultaneously, negotiations had been in progress at the DRG headquarters in Redcliffe Street, Bristol, between the company's hierarchy and the SOGAT representatives, Cliff Phillips, a national organiser, and Brian Hopton, the Bristol and the West of England assistant branch secretary. On Monday evening a formula for a return to work was agreed that lifted the suspensions imposed on members of the machine and finishing chapels; but my dismissal was excluded from this arrangement. The company had made it quite clear that they would not reinstate me. They went further and said even if ordered by an industrial tribunal they would not take me back.[212]

When clerical chapel members arrived at work on Tuesday morning to commence their strike, they would have heard the humming sound of machinery signalling the end of the stoppage. Of course, some had already heard the news. At 9.45am the clerical chapel officers gathered their members to hear, from the machine chapel FoC, George Bly, Len Stephen, and Brian Hopton, the outcome of the previous day's negotiations at Redcliffe Street. The details of the return-to-work formula agreed with the company were given to the chapel, leaving me to fight my case through an industrial tribunal.[213] Later Cliff Phillips, the SOGAT national organiser claimed that

> the FoCs were concerned the strike might crumble because of the lukewarm support from members within other sections of the DRG Group in and around Bristol. It was his opinion at that time [and subsequently] that the Company would not reinstate Mike Richardson.[214]

On hearing the news, I think Chris was more outraged and upset than I was: "what bastards they [union officers] are no courage or guts" though I did send a letter to John Jones, the chair of SOGAT Bristol and West of England branch, requesting an emergency meeting to argue that the union should revive its effort to get me reinstated. But as the strike had been called off, I was under no illusion that the union would want to raise my case again. It had already given in. However, I felt that it had to be held accountable, for I thought that if enough pressure had been put on the company, the possibility of winning reinstatement might still be open.

Over the next few days at home and alone, the consequences of my action began to sink in. Isolated from former co-workers and feeling utterly abandoned by the union bureaucracy I became dispirited. I was severely shaken after non-stop engagement with the union. That old sense I had of being an outsider, disconnected from the external world, wrapped up in my own thoughts, returned. I listened to the Simon and Garfunkel song *I am a Rock*, again and again, especially the last few lines, "I am a rock, I am an island, and a rock feels no pain, and an island never cries". I was numb as well as stranded. As the days and weeks went by, however, the emotional hurt and distress gradually receded.

On the 6th March, delegates from print workers' support groups from twelve London boroughs, along with representatives from Reading and Portsmouth, gathered in London to form the union of print workers' support groups to provide assistance to those News International workers who had been sacked. I attended in a personal capacity because by the time I became aware of this meeting it was too late to get any official accreditation from the printers' support group in Bristol of which I was a member. I was fortunate enough to get a lift there and back so there was little expense involved.

Speaker after speaker came to the rostrum calling for the building of more support groups, mass picketing of Wapping and flouting the anti-union laws. Moreover, they advocated a strike to shut down all Fleet Street newspapers. Lawrence Jenkins, a SOGAT *Daily Telegraph* Worker argued that "new technology is something that is in the interests of print workers, but only if it is under workers' control. That is the key issue all Fleet Street workers need to grasp."[215] When it was my turn, I put the case for extending support to those SOGAT members in the provinces who were also under attack from their employers. The management at Robert Maxwell's printing plant at Paulton, near Bristol had indicated that it was prepared to close the plant if it was unable to get the print unions to accept 185 job losses and a complete reorganisation of working practices by the 4th April. I also summarised the ongoing dispute at DRG FP and my dismissal.[216]

Apart from my intervention, this meeting was solely focused on the News International dispute and the challenge of new technology within the newspaper industry in Fleet Street. After the meeting, Frank Dobson, a Labour MP approached me and wished me well in my fight for reinstatement. But the majority of the delegates had quickly dispersed and the opportunity to establish a firm contact had passed.

Back in Bristol, I put my mind to our financial survival. Chris was working part-time in a low paid job. Both my daughters were living at home and still receiving their education, one at the local secondary school and the other at a local sixth form college. I signed on at the Bishopsworth office of the Department of Health and Social Security (DHSS) to claim unemployment benefit. My claim was turned down because DRG FP informed them that I had failed to take up an offer to train for a new job opportunity, so I had to wait several weeks before I qualified for any entitlement. Although I was eligible for £10 a week unemployment benefit from my union, it could not pay me because SOGAT's funds had been sequestrated as a result of its defiance of a high court injunction, obtained by Rupert Murdoch, to stop members picketing newspaper distribution centres. Instead help came from people I knew from work; hundreds of my former colleagues contributed to weekly collections to help finance me through a difficult period. This generosity covered what would have been my take home pay for four weeks. It was absolutely vital, and I will never forget it (I still have the signed contribution sheets). Not only did it mean we could eat and pay the bills, but it also reassured me that I was not alone.

I continued to play a part in the organising of and participating in the night-time picketing of W. H. Smiths' distribution centre in Bristol and the Thomas Nationwide Transport (TNT) depot (now a modern farmyard) near Chipping Sodbury. The latter was situated several miles outside of Bristol on the A46, an unlit country road fairly near the M4 motorway. Apart from the problem of transporting large numbers of people to the depot it was an ideal place to picket. There were only two entrances, about 100 yards apart. Fifty or 60 pickets were enough to block transport coming in and out. We only achieved this a few times, but it did demonstrate that we could delay the delivery of papers to the wholesalers for sorting and distribution to the newsagents.

I was present on one occasion when at around 4.30am, after failing to stop the lorry from Wapping entering the premises, 40 or 50 of us sat down in front of the gates and linked arms to prevent the exit of delivery vans loaded with morning newspapers. As quickly as the police dragged us away, we took our places again. It felt like a merry-go-round. This went on for about three quarters of an hour before police reinforcements arrived and after a few scuffles, and the toppling of one or two police helmets, the vans broke through.

A week after this event, Mike Vine and I arrived at the depot alone around 1am. We approached the gates and engaged the security guard in conversation, telling him that two coach loads of pickets from Swindon were expected soon. Of course, he had to inform the manager who had to rise from his bed and make his way to the depot. When he arrived, three quarters of an hour later, to organise the defence of his workers, Mike and I jumped in my car and left for Bristol. There were no coaches due!

On 13th March, after a long debate featuring some tetchy moments, the Bristol and the West of England branch committee approved a motion I had submitted calling on the SOGAT NEC

> to support the fight to obtain re-instatement for the FoC (branch committee member and B.D.C. [Biennial Delegate Council] who was sacked from DRG Flexible Packaging for upholding the policies of the Society and standing by the principles of Trade Unionism.[217]

The following Monday evening the clerical chapel committee assembled at Janet's home. On the basis that I was contesting my dismissal, I continued as FoC and therefore I was at this meeting. I recommended that the clerical chapel should not merge with the machine chapel because I felt it was still strong enough to operate separately. Julie Brown, the daughter of Brian, who had been made redundant, volunteered to act as temporary secretary and Mary Powell, stepped in as the representative for the accounts office.[218]

The next day Clive Pinney, a solicitor for Robin Thompson & Partners, who acted for the unions, contacted me. We met and I submitted an eleven-page document of evidence I had prepared in support of my allegation that the company had dismissed me on grounds related to my trade union activities. He took it away for editing, cut it by a few pages and returned it on the 20th for me to check and sign. He asked me to bring it to the tribunal to give to the barrister he was 'instructing'. This meant that the barrister only had around an hour to read up on my case beforehand. On his admission this was not enough time for him to fully prepare.[219] Either my union had taken too long in sending the relevant documentation or the solicitor had not given it the priority it required.

I rang Gwen, my former deputy FoC, to confirm that she would accompany me to the hearing as my witness. Later that evening, I was present at the Bristol Trades Council meeting when it passed a resolution supporting my fight for reinstatement. The Council treasurer, Don Bateman said "it is ironic that we should be discussing this matter [my dismissal] on a day that the company [DRG group] announced a 20 per cent rise in profit".[220] Don was a well-known figure in the Bristol labour movement who had written on the growth of the Bristol and its packaging industry in the nineteenth century, which included

Robinson's, as part of his PhD. This backing from the Trades Council provided me with a much-welcomed morale booster. The next day I met my barrister for the first time and we quickly went through the case.

I entered the courtroom and faced the tribunal's judicial body, the chair of the proceedings, an employment judge, an employers' association nominee, and a representative of a TUC-affiliated union. The panel were sat behind the desk on a raised platform, yet the atmosphere was not too formal. In his opening remarks the tribunal chair posed his rhetorical question:

> Why on earth should a thirty-nine-year-old man with a wife and two children, employed at the company [DRG FP] for fourteen years, take such an action without good reason?

This I interpreted as a glimmer of hope.

I was called to the witness chair and responded fairly calmly to questions put by the barristers. I cannot recall them all or my answers, but it was dawning on me that I had no cause to hope that the Tribunal chair would have any sympathy with my moral objection to taking the job of someone else who had been made redundant. He put to it me "do you really believe you can pick and choose which instructions, given by your employer, you can obey?" He went on to indicate that no matter how many union agreements between an employer and a trade union, the only legal requirement of the company was its obligations under the 1975 Employment Protection Act. These were consequently the only terms the court would consider. This, I felt, left little room for the trade union representative on the panel to argue my case.[221]

The 7th May was set for the resumption of the hearing, giving time for both parties to consider their positions. Soon after, the first hearing adjourned. Immediately after I met with my barrister in another room. He said they were "putting up a hell of a fight" but indicated we would not win. He had spoken with the employer's barrister who said that the company would agree to an out of court settlement of £2000 with no admission of my allegation. He strongly advised me to accept. I had not come this far to give up now, so I refused the offer.[222]

A week later, Brian Hopton phoned requesting that I write to Brenda Dean, SOGAT General Secretary, to acquaint her with the details of my case in preparation for the NEC's deliberation on the matter of supporting my fight for reinstatement. I sent a heavily truncated version of the statement I had given to my solicitor, Clive Pinney. I ended my letter saying that the "Company have attempted to smash the Clerical Chapel culminating with my sacking. They will not suceed (*sic*). Obviously, we have had a setback, but I was now reorganising the Chapel from outside".[223]

It was Easter week and as well as picketing TNT on Thursday, on Saturday around midnight I and around 50 other SOGAT and NGA members assembled to form a new picket line at Western Web Offset Printers Ltd in Brislington. The firm had been given a contract to print a regional edition of the *News of the World*. The police were prepared. They had placed barriers by the side of the exit road to keep back protesters. However, they allowed a few pickets to approach the van drivers as they were leaving the premises with their consignment of Murdoch's paper for distribution. The first couple of drivers stopped to listen but were not persuaded. We then broke through the barriers in an attempt to block them but were pushed back by the police. We returned every Saturday night for the next four weeks but there were not enough of us to have much of an impact.

At the end of March, I wrote to the FoCs of the SOGAT chapels at DRG FP and asked them to pass on to their members my gratitude for the financial support they had given to my family and me. I went on to say that given by 10th April I should be in receipt of unemployment benefit, so this was an appropriate time to stop the collection. "I wished them well for the future, a socialist future." I ended with this quote from Hegel, a nineteenth century philosopher.

> People have a feeling that, if thinking passes the ordinary range of our ideas and impressions, it cannot but be on the evil road. They seem to be trusting themselves to a sea on which they will be tossed to and fro by the waves of thought, till at length they again reach the sandbank of this temporal scene, as utterly poor as when they left it. What comes of such a view, we see in the world.[224]

Directly after Easter, I heard from the SOGAT General President, Danny Sergeant. He informed me that unfortunately the letter I had sent to Brenda Dean was "not read out" at the NEC meeting because the Bristol NEC member, Cliff Hall, was not present. Therefore, the case of my dismissal was handed to him to deal with.[225]

During the first week of April, I began applying for jobs within the printing industry. The printers J. W. Arrowsmith replied, but only had a vacancy for an operator on a trimmer and gathering machine, and Wiltshire printers in Bedminster said it had no immediate openings. At night I continued to fulfil my share of picketing W. H. Smith, TNT and Western Web. On Sunday the 6th, I went to a rally in London to show support for the sacked News International workers. The print unions' picket organising committee, formerly known as the printers' support group, had organised three coaches to go from the NGA office in Bristol. The contingent was made up largely of NGA members. On arriving in London, we joined several thousand others and marched from Trafalgar Square to Wapping where speeches were delivered by Norman Willis, the TUC general secretary, Tony Dubbins, the NGA general secretary, Brenda Dean, the SOGAT general secretary and John Prescott, the MP for Hull East. After the rally there was a confrontation between around 1,000 demonstrators and the police resulting in some injuries and 20 arrests. I did not witness this because, along with the Bristol contingent, I had to catch the coach we had booked to take us back home.[226]

The next morning, I called in the NGA office in Baldwin Street, in the centre of Bristol, for a meeting of the picket organising committee. As usual, there was no full-time SOGAT Bristol branch official present. The NGA Bristol branch secretary, Terry Cleverly, and his deputy, Geoff Collard, who I knew well from the time he had been employed by DRG FP, ran the meeting. They announced that there was to be a large picket on 16th April and that we should tell members and supporters to report to the NGA offices at midnight. Only then would we be told where it would take place. In the meantime, the regular pattern of picketing was to continue.

On Monday afternoon, 7th April, I reported back to the branch committee on Sunday's march and rally. I expressed my feelings about the poor turnout from our branch. I felt that at the very least committee members should have made a bigger effort to attend and said that perhaps they should have been mandated to go. I then called on them to come and support the picket lines at the distribution centres and to ask their members to join the big picket on 16th April. Mike Vine called for volunteers to join him on the following Saturday in Broadmead, Bristol, to distribute informational leaflets on the dispute. One member responded by stating "that it was a shame that the union was being destroyed on a principle of law which the General Secretary could not win." Some other members shared this view, which was probably why they were less than enthusiastic about joining picket lines and rallies.[227]

A week later, Monday 14th, I went to London to discuss my fight for reinstatement with the SOGAT general president, Danny Sergeant. Bernard Vowles and the former NATSOPA Bristol branch secretary, Joe Hall, were also present. Danny Sergeant brought Cliff Phillips with him. Cliff had negotiated the return-to-work agreement with DRG FP that left me out in the cold to pursue my case through an industrial tribunal.

Danny opened the meeting with an apology because he could only spare five minutes. Then Bernard Vowles spoke, saying that he was disgusted that I did not "get the support from SOGAT members within DRG" but that I "must be supported now." He declared having had "political differences" with me but testified nonetheless that "along with Mike Vine" I was 'the most active member on the picket lines and was the most active FoC in the Branch".[228]

Cliff Phillips defended his decision to recommend the return-to-work agreement he had negotiated. He was absolutely sure that under no circumstances would the company reinstate me. He had felt he had to move quickly because the FoCs of the machine and finishing chapels thought that backing from SOGAT FoCs representing members "within other sections of the DRG Group…was lukewarm".

In response, I argued that my "reinstatement could have been won when all the members of SOGAT were out on strike"; particularly as the clerical chapel had voted to join their factory colleagues on strike while negotiations were still in progress. I went on to contend "that passivity does not work". I gave as an example the case of the DRG Carton factory, which was put up for sale even though the FoCs had gone out of their way to help the company through difficult times by acceding to the adoption of radical changes in working practices. Danny Sergeant agreed with me, but he had run out of time and needed to conclude. In parting he promised to "take the case of re-instatement to the highest levels in the DRG group."[229] I had travelled from Bristol to London just to spend ten minutes with him and hear his meaningless gesture.

The following day I met with Bernard Vowles and Brian Hopton at the SOGAT Bristol office. They told me that Danny Sergeant had spoken with DRG's senior management and got the same response as Cliff Phillips. On his advice, Bernard then asked me whether I would give the union permission to approach ACAS to try and make a settlement with the company on the basis of accepting redundancy. I declined. Bernard accused me of being "on some kind of ego trip" and said I should reconsider because of my family, so I agreed to consult with Chris overnight.[230]

Chris left the decision to me. I returned the next day and stated that I would not take a settlement that involved redundancy, but I would consider an out of court settlement premised on unfair dismissal. Astoundingly, later that day the solicitor rang and informed me that the company had offered £9,450 compensation, provided a form of wording could be reached to satisfy both parties. A week later I received the official signed document confirming that I would receive £9,450 from the respondent (DRG) "in full and final settlement of all matters arising under any acts which fall under the jurisdiction of an industrial tribunal or otherwise arising out of the applicant's employment with the respondent or the termination thereof."[231] A bit of a fudge but good enough for me to move on. I wrote to the clerical chapel to tell them that with deep regret I had formally resigned. On 13th May 1986, Bob Palmer was elected as FoC in my place.

Meanwhile, on 6th May the SOGAT NEC decided to end the union's contempt of court. The SOGAT London District Council expressed "disgust and abhorrence" towards the leadership for taking this decision.[232] The Bristol and West of England branch went further and "urge[d] the NEC to reimpose the blacking [*sic*] of all News International titles."[233] Bernard Vowles, who was not at this meeting, challenged the motion's legitimacy. He used this "to extricate him from passing on" the branch committee's view to the NEC. His challenge was overruled "but it came too late to influence events before the start of SOGAT's biennial conference" in early June.[234]

Once my fight for reinstatement was lost, I extended my search for a job in the print industry. Bristol United Press had some clerical vacancies, so I applied but failed to get an interview. I did get a foot in the door at Her Majesty's Stationary Office (HMSO) through my branch committee colleague Tom Ovens, but no job offers materialised. Picketing and meetings occupied me in the evenings (and nights).

I accepted an invitation from Keith Mahoney, secretary of the Bristol Gas branch of the National and Local Government Officers Association (NALGO), to speak on the News International dispute at the Black Swan in Easton on 29th May. The following evening, at a public meeting "Defend our Unions, Defend our Jobs", I shared a platform at Transport House, Victoria Street with Ron Thomas, ex Bristol MP, Sian James, chair of the South Wales Women's Support Groups, and Bill Etherington, National Justice for Mineworkers Campaign and NUM executive member. Also present was a print worker on strike at Robert Maxwell's Purnell's factory in Paulton and Heather Smith, dismissed after taking strike action in a dispute at Silentnight bed factories in the north of England. Dawn Primarolo, presided. Again, I spoke on the News International dispute and my dismissal.

On Saturday 7th June I arrived in Scarborough to join hundreds of other delegates to the SOGAT Biennial Conference. Branches across the country had already discussed the agenda and motions to be put forward during the week and where appropriate had made policy decisions. Emergency motions, however, were not made available to the delegates until the conference commenced, though we knew that there would be at least one on the News International dispute. There were in fact ten but only two of them were really relevant to how the union would progress the dispute.

The London machine branch submitted the first key motion (No. 2), which condemned the NEC for ending its contempt of court. It went on to call on conference to instruct "the NEC to pursue the dispute with all vigour to defeat the anti-unionist stand of Murdoch's Multi-National Group." This constituted a plea to revitalise the support the union had gained by once more defying the law, as the expectation was that TUC affiliated unions would rally round a union whose very existence would be in jeopardy. The NEC submitted the second motion (No. 8), which agreed that the dispute would continue, but within the constraints of the law and under its direct control. However, we had to wait until Thursday, the fifth day of the conference, for the debate and vote.[235]

Behind the conference scenes, the London branches were drumming up support for the machine branch resolution and urging delegates to oppose the NEC motion. Brenda Dean summoned Bernard Vowles to tell him of her fury over the Bristol and West of England branch resolution criticising the NEC for purging their contempt of court. She was concerned that the Bristol delegation would oppose the NEC's motion. Both Mike Vine and I argued that our delegation should be mandated to vote in line with branch policy. Bernard Vowles vehemently opposed this and managed to persuade the majority of the branch delegates, some of whom had never even been on a picket line, that they should have a free vote.

Each day, outside the conference hall, a large contingent of sacked News International workers lobbied us when we entered and exited the building. They expressed feelings of anger, betrayal, and defiance because they had heard that the SOGAT leadership were prepared to let them down and beat a retreat. The graffiti displayed on the walls and around the town "Brenda Deals" dispelled any doubts about their frame of mind. From the conference platform, Brenda Dean appealed to the London branches to control their members who were, she alleged, over-zealous. She complained that she had been pushed and shoved. The atmosphere had reached fever point by the time the emergency resolutions were to be debated.

The drama created then took a surprising turn. Delegates who supported the London branches were thrown into turmoil when the London machine branch mysteriously withdrew their motion condemning the NEC's action in ending its contempt of court. This left the union's general secretary to move the NEC motion supporting the continuation of the dispute under the control of the NEC "consistent with ensuring the maintenance of SOGAT as an independent trade union". By this she meant that the dispute could only be pursued within the law. She said that before the NEC purged its contempt of court "we did have a situation of this union breaking up. Without the union we cannot help our members in News International…How on earth is that going to help our members in this dispute." She went on to say, "the NEC would not allow the courts or the sequestrators to take this union from us."

As soon as Brenda Dean and the seconder of the NEC motion had finished addressing the delegates, the London branches asked for, and were granted, a fifteen-minute adjournment to consider their position. When they returned, to everybody's surprise, they threw their support behind the NEC's resolution. Delegates from outside the London branches were shocked and confused. Mike Vine and I were among a tiny number of disaffected delegates who voted against. The NEC motion was overwhelmingly approved.[236] Brenda Dean claimed that the union would go forward united but within a few weeks she revealed her pessimism when she said the dispute was lost "when the very first newspaper lorry left the plant".[237]

On returning from the SOGAT biennial conference, I signed up with an employment agency taking warehouse work finding and extracting products to fulfil customer requirements from food distribution centres in Avonmouth and Yate. The job had changed since my days working for the Bristol Co-operative Society in the late 1960s. With the introduction of computers, the work was now timed. If you did not meet the standard required, you were fired. While doing a few days' work at one warehouse, I complained to the agency about the appalling condition of the toilet facilities. It did take up the case, but I was moved on to work for another company and never learned the outcome of my protestation.

I continued applying for jobs in the print industry and managed to get an interview at Allen Davies printing works. As I remember I was questioned about the circumstances in which I left my employment at DRG FP. Unsurprisingly, no job offer was forthcoming. Nonetheless, SOGAT did find me several weeks' temporary work at Ault & Wiborg inks at Yate near Bristol. On one occasion, during my period of employment there, I was given the task of filling 10 litre heavy duty tin pails with printing ink, fed from a tap at the base of a large vat suspended on a hoist. Once filled, I had to fasten and seal the lids, and then label with the customer's name and address.

When the vat was empty, I had to clean it out. I was not warned about the effect of toxic fumes when reaching down deep into the vat to wash it with a large brush and a cleaning solvent, which unbeknown to me was toluene based. On first carrying out this task, the affect of the toluene vapour, much to the amusement of my work colleagues, sent me into a spin and I stumbled around like a drunken man. Toluene had also been used at DRG FP in its printing inks and lacquers. In poorly ventilated areas it could cause dizziness, confusion and anxiety. It was no laughing matter. Working in an all-male environment could be challenging.

The job finished in August. But fortunately an opportunity arose at the Gwent College of Higher Education to undertake a full-time course in 'Trade Union and Social Studies', over nine months. A student grant covered a sizable part of my costs, though it did mean commuting daily from Bristol to Newport. The effort was more than compensated by the opportunity to study with, and learn from, other trade union and community activists, guided by really committed teachers.

The syllabus included labour history, industrial relations, political economy, and sociology. We were not tied to the examination system. There were no exams, and although assignments and the final dissertation were graded, this was purely done to meet the college

Trade Union & Social Studies Class, 1988, Gwent College of Higher Education, Newport.

regulations. The diploma awarded was based largely on completing the study programme and, to a marginal degree, the general assessment of the tutors. It was a profoundly important experience for me, which lifted my self-confidence and reawakened hope.

1987

By successfully completing this course, I received a college diploma in higher education. This qualification gave me the opportunity to study for a degree as a mature student at university. At this juncture in my life, however, I decided not to try for this opening. Instead, I began again to look for work in the printing industry; my aim was to become actively involved in union work again at the local level, and also to improve our family finances.

Through the union I became one of several casual workers employed by the day at Bristol United Press (BUP) working on the loading bay. If I was lucky, I was called in around three times a week to cover for holidays and sickness. The size of the paper determined the numbers of staff required each day. I had to wait at home for a phone call each morning until around nine o'clock to see if I was needed. Casuals were paid cash-in-hand at the end of each day's work, about £30 as I recall. It was heavy work on the lower ground floor. The air filled with petrol and diesel fumes when the vans backed in to pick up the *Bristol Evening Post* for distribution to the newsagents three times a day; the midday edition, the two star edition at around 3.00pm and the three-star an hour or so later.

After six months, October 1987, a permanent position became available in the pressroom. I applied. The foreman interviewed me. He asked me if I had a head for heights, as the printing presses were on three levels, and whether I had any experience working in a machine room. I was rather economical with the truth in my answer to both questions. From childhood, I have had a phobia about heights; nor had I worked as an operative or assistant in a machine room. But he must have been satisfied because I started my new job almost immediately on a wage that was more than £2000 a year higher than my earnings had been at DRG FP.

The pressroom was dirty, dusty and very noisy. My main job was to clear the waste generated from three Crabtree Vickers rotary presses on which the *Bristol Evening Post* and *Bristol Observer* were printed. I also had to keep the surrounding areas clean and compress the waste and tie it in bundles ready for removal. At the end of each print run I had to assist in removing the printing plates in readiness for the production of the next edition.

After a while I was put to work on the 'fly', the delivery end of the press, where the papers arrived cut and folded. The fly hand's first job of the day was to thoroughly clean the cutting and folding unit. I had an industrial vacuum cleaner, rags and cleaning fluid to do this job within a very cramped space. On finishing this task, I turned to help in the make ready process, feeding the paper, supplied in reel form from the lower deck, through impression cylinders, rollers and angle bars located on three levels of the press.

This operation required several workers positioned at various points on both the upper levels to nurse the paper through to the delivery end. Extreme care was taken because one was within a fraction of an inch of having one's fingers caught in the press. Finally, I worked with the rest of the team in placing the printing plates in their appropriate positions on the cylinders. When the press was rolling the fly hand's job was to remove and discard the 'spoiled' papers as they appeared at the delivery end. The machine was not stopped for me to do this task. It was kept running. We all laboured under incessant demand for speed.

The all-male environment of the pressroom was a harsh place for anyone deemed to be different in terms of their skills and abilities, as well as their mental and moral character. The time-honoured customary derision employed by the print workers at BUP was actually a cover for their own vulnerability—a cohesion that concealed their own fears of individual exposure. I was fortunate in that the publicity around my dismissal was quite well known among the men and therefore I was not unduly subjected to ridicule. But I was always acutely conscious about keeping up with the pace of work. Lacking practical experience, I did made mistakes when working on the 'fly', On several occasions these resulted in web breaks and the paper jamming the rollers that led to long delays for which I received my share of flak.

Incredibly, men were permitted to smoke even when the machines were running. One NGA machine operator used to smoke cigars and tapped off the ash onto the papers as they came off the fly. During lunch breaks we were allowed to go to the social club adjoining the BUP premises where we could buy alcoholic drinks that occasionally led to much frivolity in the pressroom afterwards. I was amazed that the company had not clamped down on this. The workplace customs were quite different from any I had known. The print unions held a fair amount of organisational control at BUP. They regulated the number of men to staff the print presses and, it was they, rather than management, who would bring in casual labour when needed in order to assist the core workers.

After the News International dispute, this organisational control began to weaken, but the full realisation of managerial power was to take a few more years to establish and the printers were among the last bastions of workplace union strength. I remained at BUP until September 1988 when I left to study for a degree in humanities at the University of the West of England. This was doable because it was still possible to get a reasonable grant as an adult student. I was more financially secure than I was after completing the course in Newport, and I was still able to do some occasional casual work at BUP during breaks in the academic year. My interest in left politics and my thirst for knowledge had been confirmed at Gwent College of Higher Education, and in my own heart I felt ready to turn towards a very different kind of world.

Afterword

After graduating I studied for a doctorate on industrial relations in the British Printing Industry between the wars, for which in 1995 I was awarded the degree of Doctor of Philosophy. Then, after several months of being employed as a porter at Southmead Hospital I managed to get part-time teaching work at the University of the West of England and eventually secured a permanent position as a lecturer and researcher in employee relations.

At DRG FP, a few months after I was dismissed, the company rewrote the New Technology agreement weakening it to the extent that all staff, union and non-union, would be obliged to use it. The union was paralysed. More redundancies followed in 1987-8, and in 1989 the Pembridge Investment Group acquired the DRG group for £697 million, in spite of opposition from its Chief Executive Moger Woolley. In light of the decline in membership it was no longer practical for the clerical chapel to continue and it closed in October 1989. Around the same time, along with other core sections of the Group, DRG FP was sold off. The DRG name was confined to the history books.

In 1991, after more than ten years of talks the SOGAT and NGA print unions merged to form the Graphical, Paper and Media Union (GPMU). Tony Dubbins was elected as its General Secretary. The defeated candidate for this post, Brenda Dean, the ex SOGAT General Secretary, moved off to become a life peer in 1993. In 2004 GPMU merged with Amicus, which had been created by a merger of the Manufacturing, Science and Finance (MSF) union and the Amalgamated Engineering and Electrical Union (AEEU) in 2001. In 2007, Amicus merged with the Transport and General Workers Union to form Unite the Union. Bernard Vowles, the ex SOGAT Bristol and West of England branch secretary, retired in the 1990s. In the 2015 general election he voted for UKIP![238]

My time as a union activist in the 1970s and 80s saw a series of transformations. These extended from the adoption of neo-liberalist policies that saw the reduction of government intervention in the economy, the growth of unemployment and inflation, and a cutback in social welfare provision. I observed inter-union divisions, the hardening stance of the state towards organised labour, and the negative impact that the introduction of new technology had had on substantial numbers of workers in the printing industry. It was sobering and discouraging to live through a period that saw the strengthening of the hand of management and a weakening trade union resistance, accompanied by the sacking and blacklisting of union activists.[239]

In retrospect, however, what those of us from that era possess is a memory that workplaces, and indeed society, had not always been so systematically stacked against workers. To younger generations the new relationships at work solidified into a norm, which over time came to appear inevitable.

As an academic I studied the changing work experiences of employees in a range of occupations in the public and private sectors across southern England from the late 1990s to 2010. Since my retirement I have been publishing pamphlets and books for the Bristol Radical History Group.

Becoming aware that there were relatively few personal accounts of experiences of rank-and-file trade union activists from the 1970s and 80s I decided to write my account. I suspect my memories will resonate with many others who were around in the trade union movement then.

But I have discovered through my own love of labour history that the past can jolt a new awareness by revealing that what exists came about because of decisions and conflicts lost or won. The shape of what is not inevitable, nor is it constant.[240]

Acknowledgements

I am beholden to my partner, Sheila Rowbotham, for her loving support, valuable advice and consummate copy-editing skills in writing this book. For their understanding and encouragement, special thanks go to my brothers, Dave and Robert Richardson, and my daughters, Amanda Metti and Jacqueline Clay.

Similarly, I am indebted to the following members of the Bristol Radical History Group. Trish Mensah and Keiron Farrow for reviewing and recommending it for publication; Barbara Segal and Richard Musgrove for proof reading; Richard Musgrove for coordinating the production process, and Richard Grove who designed the book cover and created a print ready text file. Also, I am grateful to my friend and former colleague at the University of the West of England, Andy Danford, for commenting on my penultimate draft.

Many other people have helped me by providing information in the course of researching, writing and producing this book for which I am also very grateful. I am particularly indebted to those who took the time to participate in the interviews I conducted in 2009: Brian Brown, Bob Palmer, Dave Sevier, Dave Gerrish and Derek Williams. Appreciation too goes to those I have corresponded with: Mike Davey (2009), Bob and Gwen Brain, Janet St. George and Alan Clarke (2020).

I am most thankful to Maurice Thompson for sharing his collection of DRG FP factory stock photos (photographer unknown), and the pictures he took in the 1980s and 90s, and to Bob & Gwen Brain and Janet St. George for the snapshots they provided of themselves.

The responsibility for any errors in the book are, of course, mine.

Abbreviations

AA	Automobile Association
ACAS	Advisory, Conciliation and Arbitration Service
AEEU	Amalgamated Engineering and Electrical Union
AEU	Amalgamated Engineering Union
AGM	Annual General Meeting
ASTMS	Association of Scientific, Technical and Managerial Staffs
ATUA	All Trades Union Alliance
AUEW	Amalgamated Union of Engineering Workers
BDC	Biennial Delegate Council
BIFU	Banking, Insurance and Finance Union
BPIF	British Printing Industries Federation
BUP	Bristol United Press
CND	Campaign for Nuclear Disarmament
CRS	Co-operative Retail Society
DHSS	Department of Health and Social Security
DRG	Dickinson-Robinson Group
DRG FP	DRG Flexible Packaging
EETPU	Electrical, Electronic, Telecommunications and Plumbing Union
EHD	Environmental Health Department
FBU	Fire Brigades Union
FoC	Father of the Chapel
GCHQ	Government Communications Head Quarters
GPMU	Graphical, Paper and Media Union
HMSO	Her Majesty's Stationery Office
IMG	International Marxist Group
IRA	Irish Republican Army
ISTC	Iron and Steel Trades Confederation
MoC	Mother of the Chapel
MP	Member of Parliament
MSF	Manufacturing, Science and Finance
NACODS	National Association of Colliery Overmen, Deputies and Shotfirers
NALGO	National and Local Government Officers Association
NATSOPA	National Society of Operative Printers and Assistants
NCB	National Coal Board
NDLB	National Dock Labour Board
NEC	National Executive Committee
NGA	National Graphical Association
NHS	National Health Service
NPA	Newspaper Publishers' Association

NRDC	National Retail and Distribution Certificate
NS	Newspaper Society
NUJ	National Union of Journalist
NUM	National Union of Mineworkers
OPEC	Organisation of Petroleum Exporting Countries
OU	Open University
RAC	Royal Automobile Club
RAF	Royal Air Force
RWP	Robinson Waxed Paper Company
RWP FP RWP	Flexible Packaging
SLADE	Society of Lithographic Artists, Engravers and Process Workers
SOGAT	Society of Graphical and Allied Trades
TAE	Technical, Administrative and Executive
TGWU	Transport & General Workers Union
TNT	Thomas Nationwide Transport
TUC	Trades Union Congress
UKIP	United Kingdom Independence Party
US	United States of America
USSR	Union of Soviet Socialist Republics
VDU	Visual Display Unit
WIP	Work-in-Progress
WRP	Workers' Revolutionary Party
YTS	Youth Training Scheme

Notes

1 *Bristol Evening Post*, 20 February 1986.
2 See Edward Palmer (E.P.) Thompson, *The Making of the English Working Class* (Pelican, 1982), Preface, 1963, pp. 8-13.
3 My elder brother was also educated at Lockleaze School, but he had proved good enough to be offered a free place at Queen Elizabeth's Hospital School in Bristol, which he turned down.
4 Quotes from my school reports, July 1962 and February 1963.
5 For an account of this campaign see Madge Dresser, 'Black and White On the Buses' in Ian Bild (ed.), *Placards and Pin Money: Another Look at Bristol's Other History* (Bristol Broadsides: 1986).
6 Between 1966 and 1970, NATSOPA merged with the National Union of Printing, Bookbinding and Paper Workers, becoming Division 1 of the Society of Graphical and Allied Trades (SOGAT). This merger collapsed in 1970 leading SOGAT Division 1 members to become National Society of Operative Printers, Graphical and Media Personnel but continued to call itself NATSOPA. In 1982 the two unions merged again.
7 Derek Williams interview, 15 July 2009.
8 Minutes of the SOGAT (RWP) clerical chapel meetings, May 1966–November 1970.
9 NATSOPA Bristol Branch Record Card, Branch No. 2075, Head Office No. 605420, Date of Entry, 12-04-1971.
10 Dave Sevier, email to Richardson, 27 September 2009.
11 Minutes of the NATSOPA (RWP) Clerical Chapel Meeting, 2 August 1971.
12 Cutting spools to the required size for receiving slit reels from a web of paper, film or film/foil.
13 Dave Gerrish interview, 14 October 2009.
14 Ibid.
15 *The Guardian*, 19 February 1972.
16 Minutes of the NATSOPA (RWP) Clerical Chapel Committee Meeting, 24 November 1971.
17 Ibid. 20 January 1972.
18 Ibid. 31 January 1972.
19 *Western Daily Press*, 24 July 1972.
20 *The Guardian*, 22 July 1972.
21 Minutes of the NATSOPA (RWP) Clerical Chapel Meeting, 14 November 1972.
22 Minutes of the NATSOPA (RWP) Clerical Chapel Meeting for the years 1972-3.
23 James W. Durcan, William E. J. McCarthy and George P. Redman (1983), *Strikes in Post-War Britain: A study of stoppages of work due to industrial disputes, 1946-73* (George Allen & Unwin, 1983), Appendix 2 'Political Stoppages, 1969-73'.
24 For a full account of this trial see Des Warren, *The Key to my Cell* (Living History Library, Liverpool: first published in 1982 by New Park Publications, Clapham, London). In March 2021, the court of appeal quashed the convictions of the Shrewsbury 24, overturning a miscarriage of justice after a forty-seven-year fight; see the account by Eileen Turnball, the researcher and secretary of the Shrewsbury 24 campaign in *Tribune*, 27 March 2021.
25 Minutes of the NATSOPA (RWP) Clerical Chapel Meeting, 17 October 1973.
26 Minutes of the NATSOPA (RWP) Clerical Chapel Committee Meeting, 23 October 1973.
27 See Des Warren, *The Key to my Cell* for a full account.
28 See Andy Beckett, *When the Lights Went Out: What really happened to Britain in the Seventies* (Faber and Faber, 2009), pp. 144-150.
29 Minutes of the NATSOPA (RWP) Clerical Chapel Meetings, 26 March 1974 and 2 April 1974.
30 Minutes of the NATSOPA (RWP) Clerical Chapel Committee Meeting, 16 May 1974.
31 Ibid. 20 May 1974
32 Minutes of the NATSOPA (RWP) Clerical Chapel Meeting, 4 June 1974.
33 *Bristol Evening Post*, 13 June 1974.
34 *Bristol Evening Post*, 19 June 1974; *Western Daily Press*, 20 June 1974.
35 *Daily Mirror*, 22 June 1974.
36 Minutes of the NATSOPA (RWP) Clerical Chapel Meeting, 27 October 1974.

37 Gerrish interview, 14 October 2009.
38 Minutes of the NATSOPA (DRG FP) Clerical Chapel Meeting, 21 January 1975.
39 Bob Palmer interview, 2009.
40 *Bristol Evening Post*, 6 May 1975.
41 John Gennard, *A History of the National Graphical Association* (Unwin Hyman, 1990), p. 406.
42 *The Observer*, 28 September 1975; *The Guardian*, 29 September 1975.
43 Minutes of the NGA Bristol Branch Committee, 27 October 1975.
44 Alun Beynon, *Bristol Socialist*, February 1976; *Red Weekly*, 4 March 1976.
45 Minutes of the NATSOPA (DRG FP) Clerical Chapel Meeting, 20 July 1976 & 26 October 1976.
46 Ibid. 20 July 1976.
47 Ian Archer, Spencer Jordan and Keith Ramsay, *Abstract of Bristol Historical Statistics part 2: Unemployment Statistics 1910-1997.*
48 In 1986, Moger Woolley became a member of the Society of Merchant Venturers.
49 Minutes of the NATSOPA (DRG FP) Clerical Chapel Meeting, 8 October 1976.
50 Minutes of the NATSOPA (DRG FP) Clerical Chapel Meeting, 26 October 1976.
51 See Alan Thornett, *From Militancy to Marxism: a personal and political account of organizing car workers* (Oxford: Left View Press, 1987), pp. 258-263; Alan Thornett, *Inside Cowley: Trade union struggle in the 1970s: who really opened the door to the Tory onslaught?* (London: Porcupine Press, 1998), pp. 84-87.
52 Minutes of the NATSOPA (DRG FP) Clerical Chapel Committee, 27 January 1977; Minutes of the NATSOPA (DRG FP) Clerical Chapel Meeting, 9 February 1977.
53 M. Richardson papers, 'Original hand written text of my speech', 15 March 1977.
54 Minutes of the NATSOPA (DRG FP) Emergency Chapel Meeting, 20 May 1977; NATSOPA (DRG FP) Chapel attendance book 1975-1987.
55 Minutes of the NATSOPA (DRG FP) Clerical Chapel Meeting, 14 September 1977.
56 Minutes of the NGA Bristol Branch Committee, 12 December 1977.
57 Victor Bailey, 'The First National Strike' in V. Bailey (ed.) *Forged in Fire: The History of The Fire Brigades Union* (Lawrence & Wishart: 1992), pp. 254-5.
58 *The Lessons of the Firemen's Strike*, reprinted from the *News Line*, issues dated 14 January to 26 January 1978.
59 *Liverpool Echo*, 2 May 1979.
60 Letter from B. Brown to K. Shipton 8 February 1978; Letter from K. Shipton to R. J. Johnson, 7 March 1978.
61 Minute of the meeting between K. Shipton, and June B. along with her union representative Mike Richardson, 3 November 1978.
62 Minutes of the NGA Bristol Branch Committee, 13 March 1978.
63 The Dickinson-Robinson Group Board Minutes, 24 May 1978, uncatalogued, Bristol Archives, accessed 24 July 2007.
64 Ibid. 4 August 1978.
65 Minutes of the NATSOPA (DRG FP) Clerical Chapel, AGM, 3 May 1978.
66 The *Guardian*, 7 September 1978; D. Coates, *Labour in Power: A study of the Labour Government 1974-1979* (Longman, 1980), p. 83.
67 Minutes of the NATSOPA (DRG FP) Clerical Chapel Committee Meeting, 1 September 1978.
68 The day after the conference, the ABC trial, as it became known, of Aubrey, Berry and Campbell was stopped after it had been revealed that the foreman of the jury was an ex-SAS officer.
69 *The Guardian*, 23 & 26 September 1978.
70 The *Guardian*, 4 October 1978.
71 *The Observer,* 12 November 1978; *The Times,* 13 November 1978.
72 For a full account of road haulage strike See Paul Smith, *Unionization & Union Leadership: The Road Haulage Industry* (Continuum, 2001), pp. 142-169; For a treatise that dispels the myths of 'bloody-minded' and 'greedy' workers surrounding the 'Winter of Discontent' see Tara M. Lopez, *The Winter of Discontent, Myth, Memory, and History* (Liverpool University Press, 2014).
73 Ibid. Smith p. 160.
74 *Hansard*, 6 February 1979.

75 NATSOPA (DRG FP) Chapel attendance book 1975-1987.
76 *News Line*, 7 April 1979.
77 *Socialist Challenge*, 13 March 1980.
78 Gennard, *A History of the National Graphical Association*, pp. 410-13.
79 D. J. Richards to All members of the Factory and Maintenance Departments at DRG FP, 18 April 1980.
80 *Socialist Press*, 10 September 1980.
81 D. J. Richards to All Members of the Company, 15 September 1980.
82 Minutes of the NATSOPA (DRG FP) Emergency Clerical Chapel Meeting, 24 October 1980.
83 Ibid.
84 'Voting Intention in Great Britain: 1976-present', Ipos MORI Poll, 18-19 December 1980, www. ipos.com accessed 25 May 2020.
85 Minutes of NATSOPA (DRG FP) Emergency Clerical Chapel Meeting, 25 March 1981.
86 Minutes of a meeting between Hugh Neate, Bob Brain (FoC), Mike Richardson (Deputy FoC) and the accounts office union representative, Brian James, 26 March 1981.
87 Notice from Bob Brain to Clerical Chapel Members, 26 March 1981.
88 W. J. Hall to R. Brain FoC NATSOPA clerical chapel, DRG FP, 7 May 1981.
89 NATSOPA (DRG FP) Clerical Chapel Bulletin, 22 May 1981; Minutes of the NATSOPA (DRG FP) Clerical Chapel Annual General Meeting, 2 June 1981.
90 DRG FP Minutes of Progress Meeting for WIP Control System, 12 June 1981.
91 M. Richardson to M. Carr, 23 June 1981.
92 M. Richardson to D. M. L. Jenkins, 24 June 1981.
93 M. Richardson, FoC, (on behalf of the clerical chapel committee) to non-unionists, 6 July 1981.
94 Richardson to Carr (cc W. J. Hall, NATSOPA District Secretary), 31 July 1981.
95 Minutes of NATSOPA (DRG FP) Clerical Chapel Committee, 31 July and the 3 and 4 August 1981.
96 Minutes of a meeting between Mike Richardson and Bob Brain (clerical chapel), George Bly and Keith Hallett (machine chapel) and Hugh Neate (accounts manager), 5 August 1981.
97 Richardson to Carr with a copy to W. J. Hall, 20 August 1981.
98 Richardson open letter to DRG FP chapel officers, 3 September 1981.
99 Brain to Chris Shinner, 26 August 1981.
100 Shinner to Richardson, 1 September 1981.
101 Richardson to Shinner, 2 September 1981.
102 Minutes of NATSOPA (DRG FP) Clerical Chapel Committee Meeting, 9 October 1981.
103 Richardson to Carr, 22 October 1981.
104 Carr to Richardson, 22 October 1981; Minutes of the Emergency Chapel Meeting 22 October 1981.
105 M. A. Freeman to R. Davis, Internal DRG FP memo, 27 November 1981.
106 Joe Hall to Richardson, 22 December 1981.
107 Notes on an interview I had with Joan Brown who worked in the typing pool during this period, 8 September 2009.
108 Notes on the meeting between Malcolm Carr, Sue Watson and Stuart Clack, representing the company and Mike Richardson and Bob Brain representing Gwen Cheetham, 14 January 1982.
109 Minutes of NATSOPA (DRG FP) Clerical Chapel Committee Meeting, 27 January 1982.
110 Minutes of the meeting between Geoff Haigh and Malcolm Carr for the company and Joe Hall, Mike Richardson and Bob Brain for NATSOPA, 28 January 1982.
111 Richardson to Haigh, 4 February 1982; Carr to Richardson, 4 February 1982; Notes on a meeting with Malcolm Carr, 5 February 1982; Haigh to Richardson, 10 February 1982.
112 D. J. Richards to Clerical Chapel Members, March 1982.
113 Minutes of NATSOPA (DRG FP) Clerical Chapel Committee Meeting, 24 March 1982.
114 John Selby to David Richards, 10 May 1982.
115 Richards to Selby, 12 May 1982.
116 Richards to Clerical Chapel Members, 14 May 1982.
117 Minutes of NATSOPA (DRG FP) Clerical Chapel Emergency Meeting, 2pm 18 May 1982.

118 Richards to 'Colleagues' [the whole workforce], 21 May 1982.
119 William (Joe) Hall to M. Richardson, 26 May 1982.
120 Meeting between M. Carr, S. Watson, H. Neate, C. Shinner and the clerical chapel officers Mike Richardson and Bob Brain, 8 July 1982.
121 R. J. Brain to M. Carr, 27 July 1982.
122 My report to the Clerical Chapel Committee, 18 August 1982.
123 Minutes of SOGAT (DRG FP) Clerical Chapel Emergency Meeting, 20 September 1982.
124 Richardson to Joe Selway, SOGAT Bristol and the West of England Branch Secretary, 21 September 1982.
125 NATSOPA/SOGAT (DRG FP) Clerical Chapel attendance book 1975-1987.
126 Carr to SOGAT (DRG FP) Clerical & Machine Chapel Officers, 19 November 1982.
127 Minutes of SOGAT Council Meeting, 22 November 1982.
128 Minutes of the SOGAT Clerical Chapel Emergency Meeting, 31 January 1982
129 Agreement on the introduction of New Technology between DRG FP and SOGAT, January 1983.
130 Addition to the DRG FP Survival Plan Agreements, 8 February 1983.
131 *The History of CND*, cnduk.org
132 *The Guardian*, 10 February 1983.
133 Richardson to Carr, 14 March 1983.
134 This advice preceded the implementation of the 1984 Employment Act that introduced secret pre-strike ballots.
135 See Reports of the Delegate Council Policy Conference, SOGAT 82, 1983, pp. 154-157, 163.
136 Brian Wensley and Malcolm Carr to NGA FoCs, AUEW Shop Stewards and SOGAT 82 Clerical Chapel FOCs (*sic*), 27 June 1983.
137 Richardson to the secretary of the NATSOPA Council, 16 June 1980.
138 Richardson to Wensley, 9 September 1983.
139 For an in-depth examination of this dispute see Nigel Costley, 'Collective Identity and Strategic Choice—a study of the printworkers' disputes of 1980 and 1983', thesis submitted in partial fulfillment of the requirements of the University of the West of England for the degree of Doctor of Philosophy.
140 *The Guardian*, 17, 18, 21, & 28 November 1983.
141 SOGAT Bristol and the West of England Branch Committee minutes, 5 December 1983.
142 SOGAT Bristol and the West of England Branch Committee minutes, 5 December 1983.
143 See Allyson Pollock, *The Privatisation of Our Health Care* (Verso, 2004).
144 Betty Underwood, interviewed by Viv Honeybourne in V. Honeybourne and I. Singer, *Personal Histories of the Second Wave of Feminism*, Volumes 1 & 2, p. 45.
145 SOGAT Bristol and the West of England Branch Committee minutes, 9 January 1984.
146 Richardson to Chapel Members, 28 February 1984.
147 Seumas Milne, *The Enemy Within: The Secret War against the Miners* (Pan Books, 1995, first published by Verso, 1994).
148 Minutes of the meeting between C. Shinner, H. Neate and M. Richardson And B. Brown, 12 March 1984.
149 Ibid.
150 Terry Goodman, *The History of Purnell & Sons and the British Printing Corporation* (Self-publication, 2004), pp. 239-44; SOGAT Bristol and the West of England Branch Committee minutes, 5 March 1984, 6 August 1984.
151 I am grateful to Hedley Bashforth and Andy Danford for this information.
152 *The Sun*, 15 May 1984.
153 SOGAT *Report of the Biennial Delegate Meeting*, Bournemouth 1984, p. 201.
154 Ibid., p. 196.
155 Jack London *Ode to a scab*. 'After God had finished the rattlesnake, the toad, the vampire, He had some awful substance left with which he made a scab.'
156 Ibid., pp. 204-6.
157 Richards to All Employees, 19 June 1984.

158 Minutes of SOGAT (DRG FP) Clerical Chapel AGM, 6 June 1984; SOGAT Bristol and the West of England Branch Committee minutes, 2 July 1984.
159 SOGAT Bristol and the West of England branch quarterly general meeting, 9 July 1984.
160 *The Guardian*, 4 September 1984.
161 Minutes of SOGAT (DRG FP) Clerical Chapel meeting, 26 September 1984.
162 *The Miners' Case* (Labour Research department, 01/10/Oct 1984), p. 13; *Socialist Organiser*, 4 October 1984; *Socialist Worker*, 5 March 2014.
163 Margaret Thatcher Foundation, Margaretthatcher.org
164 Political Speech Archive, ukpol.co.uk accessed 16 August 2020.
165 Arthur Scargill, president of the NUM. to *The Guardian*, 7 January 2000; *The Guardian*, 25 October 1984.
166 SOGAT Bristol and the West of England Branch Committee minutes, 5 November 1984.
167 SOGAT Bristol and the West of England Branch Committee minutes, 3 December 1984.
168 John Gennard and Peter Bain, *SOGAT: A History of the Society of Graphical and Allied Trades* (Routledge, 2005), pp. 410-412.
169 Email from Alan Clarke to Michael Richardson, 18 August 2020.
170 Minutes of SOGAT (DRG FP) Clerical Chapel Committee, 16 January 1985.
171 Minutes of the General Meeting of the SOGAT Bristol and the West of England Branch, 21 January 1985.
172 *The Guardian*, 16 January 1985.
173 Minutes of the DRG FP Works Council Meeting, 28 January 1985.
174 Minutes of the SOGAT (DRG FP) Council Meeting, 21 January 1985.
175 For example, see Rosemary Burton's article in *The Guardian*, 2 May 1984. More recent research has indicated that there is no association between computer use and miscarriage/birth defects.
176 Richardson to B. Vowles, 11 April 1985.
177 Arthur Alletson to Vowles, 29 April 1985.
178 Job Evaluation and Wages Structure Agreement, Clause 1.3, Job Evaluation Scoring, 27 January 1983.
179 Richardson to Shinner, 2 April 1985; Shinner to Richardson, 11 April 1985; Richardson to S. A. Watson (Personnel Officer), 16 April 1985; Watson to Richardson, 18 April 1985; Richardson to Watson, 22 April 1985.
180 Richardson to Alletson, 30 May 1985.
181 Minutes of the DRG FP Works Council Meeting, 3 June 1985.
182 Newspaper cutting from the *News Line*, undated (around mid-June 1985).
183 *The Guardian*, 25 May 1985.
184 Richardson to Alletson, 2 July 1985.
185 See minutes of the DRG FP Works Council Meeting, 3 June 1985.
186 Minutes of the DRG FP Works Council Meeting, 15 July 1985.
187 Jim Shaw, company director, to K. Mortimore with copies to members of the enquiry team, 12 December 1985.
188 Bristol Trades Union Council to the local branches of the NGA, SOGAT and NUJ, 5 August 1985; B. H. Vowles, SOGAT Bristol and the West of England Branch Secretary, to Richardson (delegate to the Bristol Trades Union Council), 12 September 1985.
189 Richardson to Barnes (cc Alletson, Haigh and Vowles), 3 October 1985.
190 *News Line*, 30 October 1985.
191 Alletson to Richardson, 7 November 1985.
192 Richardson to Barnes, 3 December 1985.
193 Barnes to all DRG FP employees, 22 January 1986.
194 Richardson's notes on the meeting between the company and SOGAT FoCs, 28 January 1986.
195 Meeting with the personnel assistant, Liz Griffiths, 24 January 1986.
196 Richardson notes for on the SOGAT (DRG FP) Clerical Chapel meeting, 27 January 1986.
197 Minutes of SOGAT (DRG FP) Clerical Chapel meeting, 27 January 1986.
198 Mike Richardson, 'Leadership and Mobilization: SOGAT in the 1986-87 News International

Dispute', *Historical Studies in Industrial relations (HSIR)* 5 (spring 2003), p. 74.
199 Richardson, Industrial Tribunal preparation notes, undated (March 1986).
200 Minutes of SOGAT (DRG FP) Clerical Chapel meeting 11 February 1986.
201 Christine Richardson's diary notes, second week of February 1986.
202 Alletson to Richardson, 19 February 1986.
203 DRG Group SOGAT FoCs to their members, 19 February 1986; J. Jones, chair of DRG SOGAT Imperial Chapel to all DRG Group chapels, 19 February 1986.
204 Jim Shaw, Production Director, to Richardson, 20 February 1986.
205 George Bly, SOGAT Imperial FOC to SOGAT machine chapel members, 25 February 1986.
206 Richardson to Barnes, 21 February 1986.
207 Geoff Barnes, Managing Director, to all employees of DRG FP.
208 Robin Thompson, Solicitors, notes on the Industrial Tribunal case for Richardson/M62124.
209 *Western Daily Press*, 4 March 1986; G. J. Smith, FoC DRG FP finishing chapel to B. Vowles, the SOGAT Bristol and the West of England branch secretary, 7 April 1986.
210 Minute of the resolution carried at the DRG Imperial Chapel Meeting, 2nd March 1986 in Richardson Notes, 2 March 1986.
211 Minutes of the SOGAT Bristol and the West of England Branch Committee, 3 March 1986.
212 Return to Work Agreement, DRG Flexible Packaging, 4 March 1986; Robin Thompson, Solicitors, notes on the Industrial Tribunal case for Richardson/M62124.
213 Minutes of the Emergency SOGAT Clerical Chapel Meeting, 5 March 1986.
214 Minutes of the meeting between Danny Sergeant, the General President of SOGAT, Cliff Phillips, other national and local organisers, and Mike Richardson, 14 April 1986.
215 Richardson's notes as an attendee; Richardson 'Leadership and Mobilization: SOGAT in the 1986-87 News International Dispute', p. 88.
216 Minutes of the SOGAT Bristol and the West of England Branch Committee, 3 March 1986; Richardson 'Leadership and Mobilization: SOGAT in the 1986-87 News International Dispute', p. 89; Goodman, *The History of Purnell & Sons and the British Printing Corporation*, p. 247.
217 Minutes of the SOGAT Bristol and the West of England Branch Committee, 13 March 1986.
218 Minutes of the SOGAT Bristol and the West of England Branch Committee, 17 March 1986.
219 Clive Pinney (Robin Thompson & Partners) to M. J. Richardson, 19 March 1986.
220 *Bristol Evening Post*, 21 March 1986.
221 Richardson handwritten notes on the industrial tribunal Richardson v. DRG FP case number 5728/86 & 6155/86.
222 Ibid.
223 Richardson to Brenda Dean, SOGAT General Secretary, 22 March 1986
224 Richardson to Officers of SOGAT Chapels at DRG FP, 31 March 1986.
225 Danny Sergeant, SOGAT General President to Richardson, 1 April 1986; Sergeant to Bernard Vowles, Bristol and the West of England branch secretary, 9 April 1986.
226 *The Guardian*, 7 April 1986; Minutes of the SOGAT Bristol and the West of England Branch Committee, 7 April 1986.
227 Minutes of the SOGAT Bristol and the West of England Branch Committee, 7 April 1986.
228 Minute of the meeting, re M. J. Richardson's dismissal by DRG FP, attended by SOGAT officers, D. Sergeant, C. Phillips, B. Vowles, G. Holly, J. Hall, B. Phipps, along with M. Richardson, 14 April 1986.
229 Ibid.
230 Richardson's minute of the meeting between SOGAT officers, Bernard Vowles and Brian Hopton, with Mike Richardson, 15 April 1986.
231 Advisory Conciliation and Arbitration Service, Tribunal case number 5728/86 & 6155/86, 21 April 1986.
232 Linda Melvern, *The End of the Street* (Methuen, 1986), p. 175.
233 Minutes of the SOGAT Bristol and the West of England Branch Committee, 12 May 1986.
234 Richardson 'Leadership and Mobilization: SOGAT in the 1986-87 News International Dispute', p. 87.
235 Society of Graphical and Allied Trades, *Report of the Biennial Delegate Meeting* (Scarborough,

June1986) pp. 112-3.
236 Ibid. pp. 145-8.
237 Melvern, *The End of the Street*, p. 188.
238 *The Guardian*, 16 May 2017.
239 See Dave Smith, and Phil Chamberlain, *Blacklisted: The secret war between big business and union activists* (New Internationalist Publications, 2015).
240 I am grateful to Sheila Rowbotham for her input in writing these last few paragraphs.

Bibliography

Archer, I., Jordan S., and Ramsay, K., *Abstract of Bristol Historical Statistics part 2: Unemployment Statistics 1910-1997.*

Bailey, V., 'The First National Strike' in V. Bailey (ed.) *Forged in Fire: The History of The Fire Brigades Union* (Lawrence & Wishart, 1992).

Beckett, A., *When the Lights Went Out: What really happened to Britain in the Seventies* (Faber and Faber, 2009).

Bott, A., 'The Firemen's Strike and the Struggle for Power', *Labour Review*, Vol 11 No 5 (New Series).

Coates, D., *Labour in Power: A study of the Labour Government 1974-1979* (Longman, 1980).

Dresser, M. 'Black and White on the Buses' in I. Bild (ed.) *Placards and Pin Money: Another Look at Bristol's Other History* (Bristol Broadsides, 1986).

Durcan, J. W., McCarthy, W. E. J., and Redman G. P. (1983), *Strikes in Post-War Britain: A study of stoppages of work due to industrial disputes, 1946-73* (George Allen & Unwin, 1983).

Gennard J. and Bain, P., *SOGAT: A History of the Society of Graphical and Allied Trades* (Routledge, 2005).

Gennard, J., *A History of the National Graphical Association* (Unwin Hyman, 1990).

Goodman, T., *The History of Purnell & Sons and the British Printing Corporation* (Self-publication, 2004).

Honeybourne V. and Singer, *Personal Histories of the Second Wave of Feminism*, Volumes 1 & 2.

Lopez, T. M. *The Winter of Discontent, Myth, Memory, and History* (Liverpool University Press, 2014).

Melvern, L. *The End of the Street* (Methuen, 1986).

Milne, S., *The Enemy Within: The Secret War against the Miners* (Pan Books, 1995, first published by Verso, 1994).

Pollock, A., *The Privatisation of our Health Care* (Verso, 2004).

Richardson, M., 'Leadership and Mobilization: SOGAT in the 1986-87 News International Dispute', *Historical Studies in Industrial relations (HSIR)* 5 (Spring 2003).

Smith, D. and Chamberlain, P., *Blacklisted: The secret war between big business and union activists* (New Internationalist Publications, 2015).

Smith, P., *Unionization & Union Leadership: The Road Haulage Industry* (Continuum, 2001).

Thompson, E. P. *The Making of the English Working Class* (Pelican, 1982).

Thornett, A., *From Militancy to Marxism: a personal and political account of organizing car workers* (Oxford: Left View Press, 1987).

Thornett, A., *Inside Cowley: Trade union struggle in the 1970s: who really opened the door to the Tory onslaught?* (London: Porcupine Press, 1998).

Archives

Mike Richardson Papers

Correspondence 1970 -1988

Minute of the meeting between K. Shipton, and June B. along with her union representative Mike Richardson, 3 November 1978.

Minutes of a meeting between Hugh Neate, Bob Brain (FoC), Mike Richardson (Deputy FoC) and the accounts office union representative, Brian James, 26 March 1981.

Minutes of a meeting between Mike Richardson and Bob Brain (clerical chapel), George Bly and Keith Hallett (machine chapel) and Hugh Neate (accounts manager), 5 August 1981.

Minutes of the meeting between C. Shinner, H. Neate and M. Richardson And B. Brown, 12 March 1984.

Minutes of the meeting between Geoff Haigh and Malcolm Carr for the company and Joe Hall, Mike Richardson and Bob Brain for NATSOPA, 28 January 1982.

Minutes of the NATSOPA (DRG FP) Clerical Chapel 1971-82.

Minutes of the NATSOPA (RWP) Clerical Chapel 1971-74.

NATSOPA (DRG FP) Chapel attendance book 1975-1987.

Notes on the meeting between Malcolm Carr, Sue Watson and Stuart Clack, representing the company and Mike Richardson and Bob Brain representing Gwen Cheetham, 14 January 1982.

SOGAT Bristol and the West of England Branch Committee minutes, 5 December 1983.

SOGAT Bristol and the West of England branch quarterly general meeting, 9 July 1984.

SOGAT Report of the Biennial Delegate Meeting, Bournemouth 1984.

Minutes of the SOGAT (RWP) clerical chapel, May 1966 - November 1970.

NATSOPA (DRG FP) Clerical Chapel Bulletin, 22 May 1981.

Notes on a meeting with Malcolm Carr, 5 February 1982; Haigh to Richardson, 10 February 1982.

Minutes of SOGAT Council Meeting, 22 November 1982.

New Technology Agreement between DRG FP and SOGAT, January 1983.

DRG FP Survival Plan Agreements, 8 February 1983.

Minutes of the SOGAT (DRG FP) Council Meeting, 21 January 1985.

Minutes of the DRG FP Works Council Meeting, 28 January 1985.

Job Evaluation and Wages Structure Agreement, Clause 1.3, Job Evaluation Scoring, 27 January 1983.

DRG FP Minutes of Progress Meeting for WIP Control System, 12 June 1981

Bristol Archives.

Dickinson-Robinson Group Board Minutes, 24 May 1978, uncatalogued, accessed 24 July 2007.

NGA Bristol Headquarters, 1989.

Minutes of the NGA Bristol Branch Committee

Index of Names

Index of Institutions and Organisations